2008 Pr

BEARING THE FRUIT
of the SPIRIT

*Love, Joy, Peace,
Patience, Kindness, Goodness,
Faithfulness, Gentleness,
Self Control*

GALATIANS 5:22-23

The Word Among Us Press
9639 Doctor Perry Road
Ijamsville, Maryland 21754
www.wordamongus.org

ISBN: 978-1-59325-107-9

© 2007 by The Word Among Us
All Rights Reserved

Scripture quotations are from the Revised Standard Version Bible: Catholic Edition, copyright © 1965 and 1966, and the New Revised Standard Version Bible: Catholic Edition, copyright © 1989, both by the Division of Christian Education of the National Council of the Churches of Christ in the U.S.A. All rights reserved. Used by permission.

Scripture readings from the Roman Catholic liturgical calendar are adapted for use in the United States. Celebrations of solemnities, feasts, memorials, or other observances particular to your country, diocese, or parish may result in some variation.

Compiled by Jeanne Kun

Cover design by DesignWorks

No part of this publication may be reproduced, stored in a retrieval system, or transmitted in any form by any means—electronic, mechanical, photocopy, recording or any other—except for brief quotations in printed reviews, without the prior permission of the publisher.

Printed in China

Dear Friend in Christ,

Crisp, tart apples . . . sweet, plump strawberries . . . tangy, succulent oranges—how we enjoy delicious fruit! We love savoring the rich flavors of sun-ripened cherries picked right from the tree and clusters of sweet, juicy grapes snipped from the vine. Yet producing such fruit is a long process.

A seed is planted in the ground and, with time and proper care, grows into a mature plant or tree capable of bearing fruit. In fact, the word "mature" means "complete in natural development" and "having the capacity to bear fruit." The plant or tree produces buds that flower and come to "fruition." Then the fruit itself must ripen to its fullness before it is ready to be eaten and enjoyed. Thus, to be mature also means to be ripe. Finally, it is within the fruit that new seeds lie hidden—seeds allowing the cycle of growth and fruitfulness to continue. So, too, with the fruit of the Spirit, the theme we've chosen for the 2008 Prayer Journal.

Love, joy, peace, patience, kindness, goodness, faithfulness, gentleness, self-control—the fruits of the Spirit Paul describes in Galatians 5:22-23—are brought forth by a mature Christian life. The Holy Spirit nurtures these small seeds planted in us by God's grace, and they ripen as we grow to maturity as God's sons and daughters. The fruit of the Spirit is the outgrowth and result of a life conformed to the character of Jesus.

Spiritual growth means growth in character, in holiness, in righteousness, in virtue. Reaching spiritual maturity means coming to the point that God can be seen in us.

At the beginning of each month, *Bearing the Fruit of the Spirit* features a selection from a great Christian writer, a church document, or Scripture that focuses on the fruit of the Spirit. Pondering and praying over these selections and keeping them in mind throughout the month will nurture your spiritual growth and fruitfulness.

In addition, page by page and day by day, the journal provides the Mass readings for the year. In 2008, the church is following Cycle A, with the gospel readings for the Sundays in Ordinary Time taken from the Gospel of Matthew.

At the top of each page of the journal, you will also find a Scripture verse or quotation from a saint or well-known contemporary Christian writer. Whenever possible, quotations have been selected that correspond to the feast days of the saints or special holy days and seasons in the liturgical year.

Keeping a prayer journal can help you recognize as well as remember how God's Spirit is at work to produce the fruit of the Spirit in you. Noting Scripture passages that seem to "speak" directly to you can help you identify the ways in which God is bringing you to maturity in his Son, Jesus. Recording your resolutions can reinforce your commitment to respond to God and to the word he speaks to you. Jotting down your struggles and triumphs—or your petitions and how God has answered them—gives you a concrete reminder of God's power, faithfulness, and mercy. Perhaps you'd like to compose your own prayers to express your deepest longings to the Lord and your gratitude for the growth and fruit you see in your life. Or you might want to simply write about your daily circumstances, feelings, and temptations, in order to face them truthfully and gain spiritual perspective on them. Since a prayer journal is private—an exchange between you and God not meant to be read by others—you don't have to "put up a good front" but can be thoroughly open and honest with God and with yourself.

Using a prayer journal is an aid and encouragement to pray faithfully each day. It is a good idea to keep the journal with your Bible so you have it close at hand during your daily time of prayer.

As you remain connected to Christ through daily prayer, through reading and meditating on Scripture, and through the sacraments, may the fruit of the Spirit mature and ripen in you.

The Word Among Us Press

Abbreviations of Books of the Bible

Acts Acts of the Apostles

Am Amos

Bar Baruch

1 Chr
1 Chronicles

2 Chr
2 Chronicles

Col Colossians

1 Cor
1 Corinthians

2 Cor
2 Corinthians

Dn Daniel

Dt Deuteronomy

Eccl Ecclesiastes

Eph Ephesians

Est Esther

Ex Exodus

Ez Ezekiel

Ezr Ezra

Gal Galatians

Gn Genesis

Hab Habakkuk

Heb Hebrews

Hg Haggai

Hos Hosea

Is Isaiah

Jas James

Jb Job

Jdt Judith

Jer Jeremiah

Jgs Judges

Jl Joel

Jn John

1 Jn 1 John

2 Jn 2 John

3 Jn 3 John

Jon Jonah

Jos Joshua

Jude Jude

1 Kgs 1 Kings

2 Kgs 2 Kings

Lam Lamentations

Lk Luke

Lv Leviticus

Mal Malachi

1 Mc 1 Maccabees

2 Mc 2 Maccabees

Mi Micah

Mk Mark

Mt Matthew

Na Nahum

Neh Nehemiah

Nm Numbers

Ob Obadiah

Phil Philippians

Phlm Philemon

Prv Proverbs

Ps Psalms

1 Pt 1 Peter

2 Pt 2 Peter

Rom Romans

Ru Ruth

Rv Revelation

Sg Song of Songs

Sir Sirach

1 Sm 1 Samuel

2 Sm 2 Samuel

Tb Tobit

1 Thes
1 Thessalonians

2 Thes
2 Thessalonians

Ti Titus

1 Tm 1 Timothy

2 Tm 2 Timothy

Wis Wisdom

Zec Zechariah

Zep Zephaniah

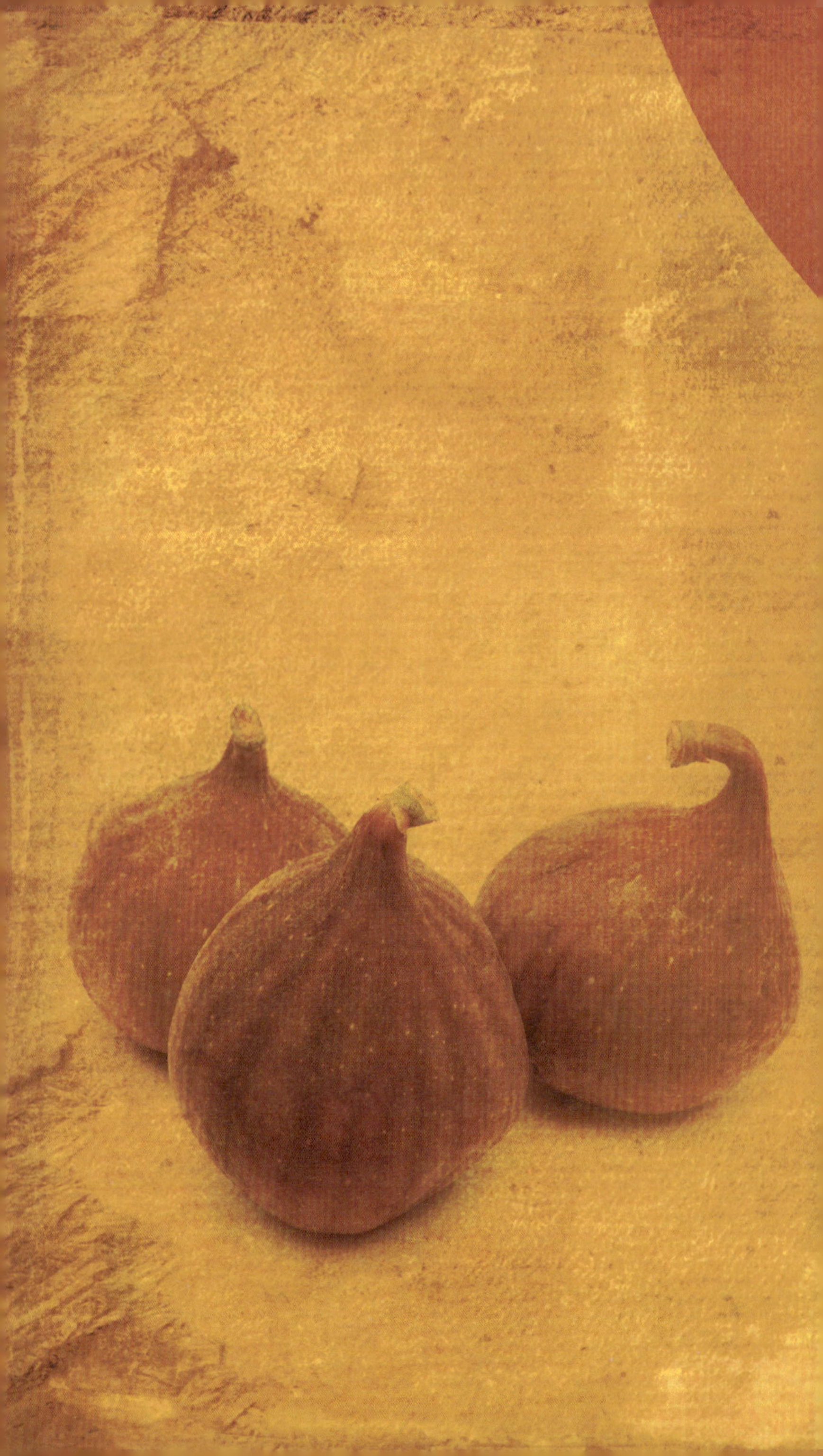

January

Perfect love means putting up with other people's shortcomings, feeling no surprise at their weaknesses, finding encouragement even in the slightest evidence of good qualities in them.

—St. Therese of Lisieux

[Mary's] task as Mother of God and mother of humans has always been to lead her human children to her divine Son.
—Catherine Doherty

1 Tuesday
Blessed Virgin Mary, Mother of God
Holy Day of Obligation
• Nm 6:22-27 • Ps 67:2-3, 5-6, 8 • Gal 4:4-7 • Lk 2:16-21

2 Wednesday
Saint Basil the Great and Saint Gregory Nazianzen
• 1 Jn 2:22-28 • Ps 98:1-4 • Jn 1:19-28

How great is your name, O Lord! When my strength fails, and darkness invades my soul, your name is the sun whose rays give light and also warmth.
—St. Faustina Kowalska

The Most Holy Name of Jesus
- 1 Jn 2:29–3:6 • Ps 98:1, 3c-6 • Jn 1:29-34

3 Thursday

Saint Elizabeth Ann Seton
- 1 Jn 3:7-10 • Ps 98:1, 7-9 • Jn 1:35-42

4 Friday

January

The Magi gaze in deep wonder at what they see: . . . man in God, God in man, one whom the whole universe cannot contain now enclosed in a tiny body.

—St. Peter Chrysologus

5 Saturday
Saint John Neumann
- 1 Jn 3:11-21 • Ps 100:1b-5 • Jn 1:43-51

6 Sunday
The Epiphany of the Lord
- Is 60:1-6 • Ps 72:1-2, 7-8, 10-13 • Eph 3:2-3a, 5-6 • Mt 2:1-12

May God shelter you from disturbance in the hidden recesses of his love, until he brings you at last into that place of fullness where you will repose forever in the vision of peace.

—St. Raymond of Peñafort

Saint Raymond of Peñafort
- 1 Jn 3:22–4:6 • Ps 2:7b-8, 10-12a • Mt 4:12-17, 23-25

7 Monday

- 1 Jn 4:7-10 • Ps 72:1-4, 7-8 • Mk 6:34-44

8 Tuesday

January

*No man has ever seen God; if we love one another,
God abides in us and his love is perfected in us.*

—1 John 4:12

9
Wednesday

- 1 Jn 4:11-18 • Ps 72:1-2, 10, 12-13 • Mk 6:45-52

10
Thursday

- 1 Jn 4:19–5:4 • Ps 72:1-2, 14-15, 17 • Lk 4:14-22a

The Son of God has come and has given us understanding to know him who is true.

—1 John 5:20

• 1 Jn 5:5-13 • Ps 147:12-15, 19-20 • Lk 5:12-16

11
Friday

• 1 Jn 5:14-21 • Ps 149:1-6a, 9b • Jn 3:22-30

12
Saturday

January

*Let us be buried with Christ by baptism to rise with him;
let us go down with him to be raised with him;
and let us rise with him to be glorified with him.*
—St. Gregory Nazianzen

13 Sunday

The Baptism of the Lord
- Is 42:1-4, 6-7 • Ps 29:1-4, 9-10 • Acts 10:34-38 • Mt 3:13-17

14 Monday

- 1 Sm 1:1-8 • Ps 116:12-19 • Mk 1:14-20

He set my feet upon a rock, making my steps secure.
—Psalm 40:2

• 1 Sm 1:9-20 • (Ps) 1 Sm 2:1, 4-8 • Mk 1:21-28

15
TUESDAY

• 1 Sm 3:1-10, 19-20 • Ps 40:2, 5, 7-10 • Mk 1:29-39

16
WEDNESDAY

JANUARY

He who knows himself knows all men.
He who can love himself, loves all men.
—St. Anthony

17 Thursday

SAINT ANTHONY
- 1 Sm 4:1-11 • Ps 44:10-11, 14-15, 24-25 • Mk 1:40-45

18 Friday

- 1 Sm 8:4-7, 10-22a • Ps 89:16-19 • Mk 2:1-12

*Grace to you and peace from God our Father
and the Lord Jesus Christ.*

—1 Corinthians 1:3

• 1 Sm 9:1-4, 17-19; 10:1a • Ps 21:2-7 • Mk 2:13-17

19
Saturday

Second Sunday in Ordinary Time
• Is 49:3, 5-6 • Ps 40:2, 4, 7-10 • 1 Cor 1:1-3 • Jn 1:29-34

20
Sunday

JANUARY

Christ will guard his own.
—St. Agnes

21 Monday

Saint Agnes
- 1 Sm 15:16-23 • Ps 50:8-9, 16b-17, 21, 23 • Mk 2:18-22

22 Tuesday

Saint Vincent
- 1 Sm 16:1-13 • Ps 89:20-22, 27-28 • Mk 2:23-28

To love our neighbor in charity is to love God in man.
—St. Francis de Sales

• 1 Sm 17:32-33, 37, 40-51 • Ps 144:1b-2, 9-10 • Mk 3:1-6

23
Wednesday

Saint Francis de Sales
• 1 Sm 18:6-9; 19:1-7 • Ps 56:2-3, 9-13 • Mk 3:7-12

24
Thursday

January

Guard the truth that has been entrusted to you by the Holy Spirit who dwells within us.

—2 Timothy 1:14

25 Friday
The Conversion of Saint Paul, Apostle
• Acts 22:3-16 or 9:1-22 • Ps 117:1b-2 • Mk 16:15-18

26 Saturday
Saint Timothy and Saint Titus
• 2 Tm 1:1-8 or Ti 1:1-5 • Ps 96:1-3, 7-8a, 10 • Mk 3:20-21

No man truly has joy unless he lives in love.
—St. Thomas Aquinas

Third Sunday in Ordinary Time
• Is 8:23–9:3 • Ps 27:1, 4, 13-14 • 1 Cor 1:10-13, 17 • Mt 4:12-23

27 Sunday

Saint Thomas Aquinas
• 2 Sm 5:1-7, 10 • Ps 89:20-22, 25-26 • Mk 3:22-30

28 Monday

JANUARY

[Jesus said:] "Whoever does the will of God is my brother, and sister, and mother."

—Mark 3:35

29 Tuesday
• 2 Sm 6:12b-19 • Ps 24:7-10 • Mk 3:31-35

30 Wednesday
• 2 Sm 7:4-17 • Ps 89:4-5, 27-30 • Mk 4:1-20

See that no one finds you motivated by impetuosity or willfulness.
—St. John Bosco

Saint John Bosco
- 2 Sm 7:18-19, 24-29 • Ps 132:1-5, 11-14 • Mk 4:21-25

31 Thursday

JANUARY

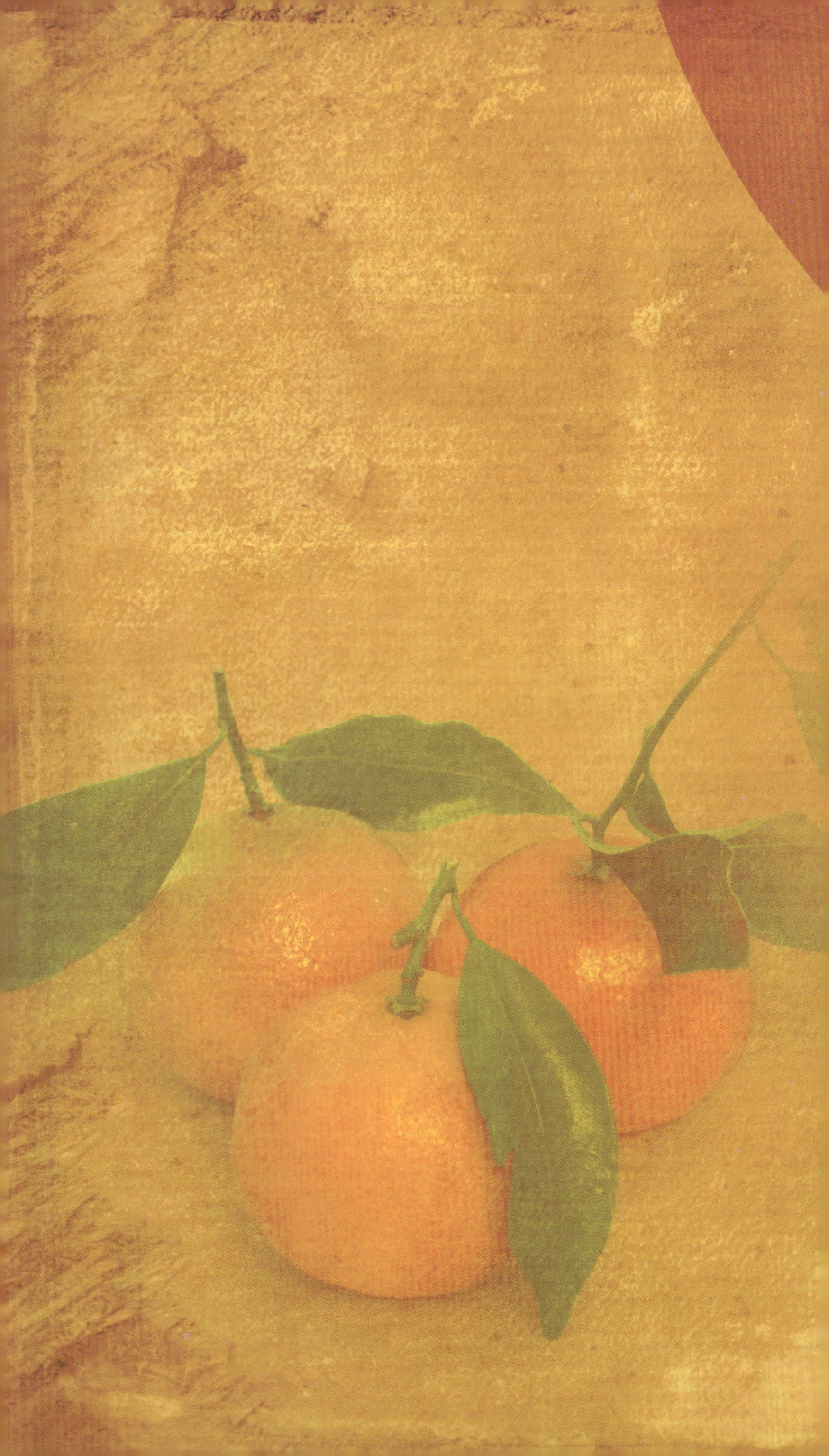

February

Are grapes gathered from thorns, or figs from thistles? So, every sound tree bears good fruit, but the bad tree bears evil fruit. A sound tree cannot bear evil fruit, nor can a bad tree bear good fruit.

—Matthew 7:16-18

> *We, too, may look for the great grace that was granted Simeon. He has shown us how to prepare for and merit it. The desire of our hearts should be to see Jesus.*
> — EDWARD LEEN, CSSp

1 — Friday
- 2 Sm 11:1-10a, 13-17 • Ps 51:3-7, 10-11 • Mk 4:26-34

2 — Saturday
The Presentation of the Lord
- Mal 3:1-4 • Ps 24:7-10 • Heb 2:14-18 • Lk 2:22-40

FEBRUARY

Blessed are the pure in heart, for they shall see God.
—Matthew 5:8

Fourth Sunday in Ordinary Time
- Zep 2:3; 3:12-13 • Ps 146:6-10 • 1 Cor 1:26-31 • Mt 5:1-12a

3 Sunday

- 2 Sm 15:13-14, 30; 16:5-13 • Ps 3:2-7 • Mk 5:1-20

4 Monday

Jesus Christ, Lord of all . . . I am your sheep: make me worthy to overcome the devil.
—St. Agatha

5 Tuesday — Saint Agatha
- 2 Sm 18:9-10, 14b, 24-25a, 30–19:3 • Ps 86:1-6 • Mk 5:21-43

6 Wednesday — Ash Wednesday
- Jl 2:12-18 • Ps 51:3-6b, 12-14, 17 • 2 Cor 5:20–6:2
- Mt 6:1-6, 16-18

FEBRUARY

When a person loves another dearly, he desires strongly to be close to the other: therefore, why be afraid to die? Death brings us to God!
—St. Josephine Bakhita

• Dt 30:15-20 • Ps 1:1-4, 6 • Lk 9:22-25

7
Thursday

Saint Jerome Emiliani; Saint Josephine Bakhita
• Is 58:1-9a • Ps 51:3-6b, 18-19 • Mt 9:14-15

8
Friday

Lent is a privileged time of interior pilgrimage towards him who is the fount of mercy.
—Pope Benedict XVI

9
Saturday
- Is 58:9b-14 • Ps 86:1-6 • Lk 5:27-32

10
Sunday

First Sunday of Lent
- Gn 2:7-9; 3:1-7 • Ps 51:3-6, 12-13, 17
- Rom 5:12-19 • Mt 4:1-11

February

Grant, most tender of mothers, that I may be a child after your own heart and that of your divine Son.
—St. Bernadette Soubirous

Our Lady of Lourdes
• Lv 19:1-2, 11-18 • Ps 19:8-10, 15 • Mt 25:31-46

11 Monday

• Is 55:10-11 • Ps 34:4-7, 16-19 • Mt 6:7-15

12 Tuesday

I give you thanks, O Lord, with my whole heart.
—Psalm 138:1

13
Wednesday

- Jon 3:1-10 • Ps 51:3-4, 12-13, 18-19 • Lk 11:29-32

14
Thursday

Saint Cyril and Saint Methodius
- Est C:12, 14-16, 23-25 • Ps 138:1-3, 7c-8 • Mt 7:7-12

FEBRUARY

> *Live in such a way that all may know that you bear outwardly as well as inwardly the image of Christ crucified, the model of all gentleness and mercy.*
> —St. Paul of the Cross

- Ez 18:21-28 • Ps 130:1-8 • Mt 5:20-26

15 Friday

- Dt 26:16-19 • Ps 119:1-2, 4-5, 7-8 • Mt 5:43-48

16 Saturday

During Lent we shall . . . with deep feeling meditate on the passion of our Lord and examine our conscience on what sin of ours caused that special pain to Jesus.
—Blessed Teresa of Calcutta

17 Sunday

Second Sunday of Lent
• Gn 12:1-4a • Ps 33:4-5, 18-20, 22 • 2 Tm 1:8b-10 • Mt 17:1-9

18 Monday

• Dn 9:4b-10 • Ps 79:8-11, 13 • Lk 6:36-38

February

> *[Jesus said:] "Whoever exalts himself will be humbled, and whoever humbles himself will be exalted."*
> —Matthew 23:12

- Is 1:10, 16-20 • Ps 50:8-9, 16b-17, 21, 23 • Mt 23:1-12

19 Tuesday

- Jer 18:18-20 • Ps 31:5-6, 14-16 • Mt 20:17-28

20 Wednesday

*Each one of the faithful is, so to speak,
the church in miniature.*
—St. Peter Damian

21 Thursday
Saint Peter Damian
- Jer 17:5-10 • Ps 1:1-4, 6 • Lk 16:19-31

22 Friday
The Chair of Saint Peter, Apostle
- 1 Pt 5:1-4 • Ps 23:1-6 • Mt 16:13-19

February

Give way to one another in the Lord's own spirit of courtesy, treating no one as inferior.
—St. Polycarp

Saint Polycarp
- Mi 7:14-15, 18-20 • Ps 103:1-4, 9-12 • Lk 15:1-3, 11-32

23 Saturday

Third Sunday of Lent
- Ex 17:3-7 • Ps 95:1-2, 6-9 • Rom 5:1-2, 5-8 • Jn 4:5-42

24 Sunday

As a deer longs for flowing streams, so my soul longs for you, O God. My soul thirsts for God, for the living God.
—Psalm 42:1-2

25 Monday • 2 Kgs 5:1-15b • Ps 42:2-3; 43:3-4 • Lk 4:24-30

26 Tuesday • Dn 3:25, 34-43 • Ps 25:4-9 • Mt 18:21-35

FEBRUARY

May our guide and teacher in our Lenten journey be Mary, most holy, who followed Jesus with total faith when he set out with determination for Jerusalem, to suffer the passion.
—POPE BENEDICT XVI

- Dt 4:1, 5-9 • Ps 147:12-13, 15-16, 19-20 • Mt 5:17-19

27 WEDNESDAY

- Jer 7:23-28 • Ps 95:1-2, 6-9 • Lk 11:14-23

28 THURSDAY

One can reach heaven from any place on earth.
—St. Samthann

29 Friday

- Hos 14:2-10 • Ps 81:6c-11b, 14, 17 • Mk 12:28-34

FEBRUARY

*We are born to love, we live to love,
and we will die to love still more.*
—St. Joseph Cafasso

March

*True peace is born of doing the will of God
and bearing with patience the sufferings of this life,
and does not come from following one's own whim
or selfish desire, for this always brings not peace
and serenity, but disorder and discontent.*

—Blessed John XXIII

The LORD is my shepherd, I shall not want.
—PSALM 23:1

1
SATURDAY
- Hos 6:1-6 • Ps 51:3-4, 18-21b • Lk 18:9-14

2
SUNDAY
FOURTH SUNDAY OF LENT
- 1 Sm 16:1b, 6-7, 10-13a • Ps 23:1-6 • Eph 5:8-14 • Jn 9:1-41

Let your heart delight in the love your God has for you, personally, individually.
—St. Katharine Drexel

Saint Katharine Drexel
• Is 65:17-21 • Ps 30:2, 4-6, 11-13b • Jn 4:43-54

3 Monday

Saint Casimir
• Ez 47:1-9, 12 • Ps 46:2-3, 5-6, 8-9 • Jn 5:1-16

4 Tuesday

March

*Abandon yourself utterly for the love of God,
and in this way you will become truly happy.*
—Blessed Henry Suso

5 Wednesday • Is 49:8-15 • Ps 145:8-9, 13c-14, 17-18 • Jn 5:17-30

6 Thursday • Ex 32:7-14 • Ps 106:19-23 • Jn 5:31-47

Just as water extinguishes fire, so love wipes away sin.
—St. John of God

Saint Perpetua and Saint Felicity
• Wis 2:1a, 12-22 • Ps 34:17-21, 23 • Jn 7:1-2, 10, 25-30

7
Friday

Saint John of God
• Jer 11:18-20 • Ps 7:2-3, 9b-12 • Jn 7:40-53

8
Saturday

March

Lent invites us to follow Christ in the mystery of his prayer, source of light and strength in time of trial.
—Pope John Paul II

9 Sunday
Fifth Sunday of Lent
- Ez 37:12-14 • Ps 130:1-8 • Rom 8:8-11 • Jn 11:1-45

10 Monday
- Dn 13:1-9, 15-30, 33-62 • Ps 23:1-6 • Jn 8:1-11

[Jesus said:] "If you continue in my word, you are truly my disciples, and you will know the truth, and the truth will make you free."

—John 8:31-32

• Nm 21:4-9 • Ps 102:2-3, 16-21 • Jn 8:21-30

11 Tuesday

• Dn 3:14-20, 91-92, 95 • (Ps) Dn 3:52-56 • Jn 8:31-42

12 Wednesday

March

To love God is to will what he wills.
—Venerable Charles de Foucauld

13 **Thursday** • Gn 17:3-9 • Ps 105:4-9 • Jn 8:51-59

14 **Friday** • Jer 20:10-13 • Ps 18:2-7 • Jn 10:31-42

Love St. Joseph with all your soul, because he, together with Jesus, is the person who has most loved our Blessed Lady and has been closest to God.
—St. Josemaría Escrivá

Saint Joseph, Husband of the Blessed Virgin Mary

- 2 Sm 7:4-5a, 12-16 • Ps 89:2-5, 27, 29 • Rom 4:13, 16-18, 22
- Mt 1:16, 18-21, 24a or Lk 2:41-51a

15 Saturday

Palm Sunday of the Lord's Passion

- Mt 21:1-11 • Is 50:4-7 • Ps 22:8-9, 17-20, 23-24
- Phil 2:6-11 • Mt 26:14–27:66 or 27:11-54

16 Sunday

MARCH

Reflect on the passion of Our Lord Jesus Christ and his precious wounds, and you will experience great consolation.
—St. John of God

17 Monday

Monday of Holy Week
- Is 42:1-7 • Ps 27:1-3, 13-14 • Jn 12:1-11

18 Tuesday

Tuesday of Holy Week
- Is 49:1-6 • Ps 71:1-6b, 15, 17 • Jn 13:21-33, 36-38

Why object to the Son of God made man washing external dirt from feet, when he who is God had already humbled himself in order to wash foulness from souls?
—Archbishop Fulton J. Sheen

Wednesday of Holy Week
• Is 50:4-9a • Ps 69:8-10, 21-22, 31, 33-34 • Mt 26:14-25

19 Wednesday

Holy Thursday
• Ex 12:1-8, 11-14 • Ps 116:12-13, 15-18
• 1 Cor 11:23-26 • Jn 13:1-15

20 Thursday

MARCH

*Savior, your crucifixion marked the end of your mortal life;
teach us to crucify ourselves and make way
for our life in the Spirit.*
—St. Ephrem

21 Friday
Good Friday of the Lord's Passion
- Is 52:13–53:12 • Ps 31:2, 6, 12-13, 15-17, 25
- Heb 4:14-16; 5:7-9 • Jn 18:1–19:42

22 Saturday
Holy Saturday
- Gn 1:1–2:2 • Gn 22:1-18 • Ex 14:15–15:1 • Is 54:5-14
- Is 55:1-11 • Bar 3:9-15, 32–4:4 • Ez 36:16-17a, 18-28
- Rom 6:3-11 • Mt 28:1-10

The Resurrection of Jesus is the crowning truth of our faith in Christ.

—Catechism of the Catholic Church, 638

Easter Sunday: The Resurrection of the Lord
- Acts 10:34a, 37-43 • Ps 118:1-2, 16-17, 22-23
- Col 3:1-4 or 1 Cor 5:6b-8 • Jn 20:1-9 or Mt 28:1-10

23 Sunday

Monday in the Octave of Easter
- Acts 2:14, 22-33 • Ps 16:1-2a, 5, 7-11 • Mt 28:8-15

24 Monday

MARCH

Easter is a feast of joy—the joy of the Lord. Let nothing so disturb us, so fill us with sorrow or discouragement, as to make us forfeit the joy of the resurrection.

—Blessed Teresa of Calcutta

25 Tuesday

- Acts 2:36-41 • Ps 33:4-5, 18-20, 22 • Jn 20:11-18

26 Wednesday

- Acts 3:1-10 • Ps 105:1-4, 6-9 • Lk 24:13-35

*Evil does not have the last word.
Christ, crucified and risen, has triumphed.*
—Pope Benedict XVI

• Acts 3:11-26 • Ps 8:2ab, 5-9 • Lk 24:35-48

27
Thursday

• Acts 4:1-12 • Ps 118:1-2, 4, 22-27a • Jn 21:1-14

28
Friday

March

Steep is the great highway I must travel, but I fear nothing, for the pure fount of mercy is flowing for my sake, and, with it, strength for the humble soul.

—St. Faustina Kowalska

29 Saturday

• Acts 4:13-21 • Ps 118:1, 14-21 • Mk 16:9-15

30 Sunday

Divine Mercy Sunday

• Acts 2:42-47 • Ps 118:2-4, 13-15, 22-24
• 1 Pt 1:3-9 • Jn 20:19-31

We Need Your Help!

Dear Friend in Christ,

Below is a survey form to help us improve future editions of the *Prayer Journal*. We need you to tell us what we are doing right or wrong and whether the *Journal* is really encouraging you in your prayer or drawing you closer to the Lord. Could you take a moment and tell us what you think of this year's *Prayer Journal*? In gratitude for your completed survey, we will take 10% off the price of the *Prayer Journal* for the next year!

1) Did you like the theme of this year's *Prayer Journal*? What two or three themes would you like to see in the future?

   _____
   _____
   _____

2) How do you use your *Prayer Journal*? (Check off one or more below.)

   ☐ To plan my day
   ☐ To recall what I learned in prayer
   ☐ As a priority-list notebook
   ☐ To take notes on spiritual matters
   ☐ Other

3) List any additional features you would like to see added to next year's *Prayer Journal*.

   _____
   _____
   _____

4) Do you use the *Prayer Journal's* companion book, called *Abide in My Word: Mass Readings at Your Fingertips*?

   ☐ Yes   ☐ No

Thank you for completing our survey. To reserve next year's *Prayer Journal* at the reduced price, complete the form below and return to:

Prayer Journal Survey
The Word Among Us
9639 Doctor Perry Road, #126N
Ijamsville, MD 21754-9900

☐ **YES!** Reserve _____ copies of next year's *Prayer Journal*. I understand that I will receive 10% off each copy and therefore pay only $12.56 each plus shipping and handling. I will not be billed until I receive my *Prayer Journal* in fall 2008.

JPRAY9

☐ **YES!** In addition, reserve _____ copies of next year's *Abide in My Word: Mass Readings at Your Fingertips*. I will receive 10% off each copy, therefore paying only $14.85 each plus s&h.

BABDE9

Name
Address
City
State   Zip
Country
Phone (   )
E-mail

NOTE: Only surveys returned by May 31, 2008 will be eligible for this discount.

QUESTIONS?
Call *The Word Among Us* Customer Service at 1-800-775-WORD (9673) if you have any questions about this discount offer.

SHIPPING & HANDLING (Add to total product order):			
If your subtotal is: $0-15	$16-$35	$36-50	$51-75
Add shipping of: $5	$7	$9	$11

CPPJ8S

Our Lady was full of God because she lived for God alone, yet she thought of herself only as the handmaid of the Lord. Let us do the same.

—Blessed Teresa of Calcutta

The Annunciation of the Lord

• Is 7:10-14; 8:10 • Ps 40:7-11 • Heb 10:4-10 • Lk 1:26-38

31 Monday

MARCH

April

We need to love our neighbor, not just because he is pleasant or helpful or rich or influential or even because he shows us gratitude. These motives are too self-serving. . . . Genuine love rises above creatures and soars up to God. In him, by him, and through him it loves all men, both good and wicked, friends and enemies.

—St. Maximilian Kolbe

*In the trials and temptations we face regularly
in our daily lives, help one another.*
—St. Francis of Paola

1
Tuesday

- Acts 4:32-37 • Ps 93:1-2, 5 • Jn 3:7b-15

2
Wednesday

SAINT FRANCIS OF PAOLA
- Acts 5:17-26 • Ps 34:2-9 • Jn 3:16-21

APRIL

> *Reading the holy Scriptures . . . turns man's attention from the follies of the world and leads him to the love of God.*
> —St. Isidore of Seville

• Acts 5:27-33 • Ps 34:2, 9, 17-20 • Jn 3:31-36

3 Thursday

Saint Isidore
• Acts 5:34-42 • Ps 27:1, 4, 13-14 • Jn 6:1-15

4 Friday

*When the soul has seen God, what more can it want?
If it possesses him, why and for whom
can it ever be moved to abandon him?*
—St. Vincent Ferrer

5 Saturday — Saint Vincent Ferrer
• Acts 6:1-7 • Ps 33:1-2, 4-5, 18-19 • Jn 6:16-21

6 Sunday — Third Sunday of Easter
• Acts 2:14, 22-33 • Ps 16:1-2, 5, 7-11
• 1 Pt 1:17-21 • Lk 24:13-35

APRIL

Show your love for those whom God has given you, just as Christ loved the church.
—St. John Baptist de la Salle

Saint John Baptist de la Salle
- Acts 6:8-15 • Ps 119:23-24, 26-27, 29-30 • Jn 6:22-29

7 Monday

- Acts 7:51–8:1a • Ps 31:3c-4, 6-8a, 17, 21ab • Jn 6:30-35

8 Tuesday

[Jesus said:] "I am the bread of life; he who comes to me shall not hunger, and he who believes in me shall never thirst."

—John 6:35

9 Wednesday
- Acts 8:1b-8 • Ps 66:1-7a • Jn 6:35-40

10 Thursday
- Acts 8:26-40 • Ps 66:8-9, 16-17, 20 • Jn 6:44-51

April

> *Be kind, be kind, and you will be saints.*
> —Blessed Jan van Ruysbroeck

Saint Stanislaus
- Acts 9:1-20 • Ps 117:1-2 • Jn 6:52-59

11 Friday

- Acts 9:31-42 • Ps 116:12-17 • Jn 6:60-69

12 Saturday

Your peace shall be in much patience.
—Thomas à Kempis

13 SUNDAY

Fourth Sunday of Easter
• Acts 2:14a, 36-41 • Ps 23:1-6 • 1 Pt 2:20b-25 • Jn 10:1-10

14 MONDAY

• Acts 11:1-18 • Ps 42:2-3; 43:3-4 • Jn 10:11-18

APRIL

> *May God be gracious to us and bless us and make his face to shine upon us.*
> —Psalm 67:1

• Acts 11:19-26 • Ps 87:1b-7 • Jn 10:22-30

15 Tuesday

• Acts 12:24–13:5a • Ps 67:2-3, 5-6, 8 • Jn 12:44-50

16 Wednesday

We must aim at heaven with all our strength.
—Alfred Delp, SJ

17 Thursday • Acts 13:13-25 • Ps 89:2-3, 21-22, 25, 27 • Jn 13:16-20

18 Friday • Acts 13:26-33 • Ps 2:6-11b • Jn 14:1-6

APRIL

> *O sing to the Lord a new song,
> for he has done marvelous things!*
> —Psalm 98:1

• Acts 13:44-52 • Ps 98:1-4 • Jn 14:7-14

19 Saturday

Fifth Sunday of Easter
• Acts 6:1-7 • Ps 33:1-2, 4-5, 18-19 • 1 Pt 2:4-9 • Jn 14:1-12

20 Sunday

*Speak now, my heart, and say to God,
"I seek your face; your face, Lord, I seek."*
—St. Anselm

**21
Monday**

Saint Anselm
• Acts 14:5-18 • Ps 115:1-4, 15-16 • Jn 14:21-26

**22
Tuesday**

• Acts 14:19-28 • Ps 145:10-13b, 21 • Jn 14:27-31a

April

> *[Jesus said:] "He who abides in me, and I in him, he it is that bears much fruit, for apart from me you can do nothing."*
> —John 15:5

Saint George; Saint Adalbert
- Acts 15:1-6 • Ps 122:1-5 • Jn 15:1-8

23 Wednesday

Saint Fidelis of Sigmaringen
- Acts 15:7-21 • Ps 96:1-3, 10 • Jn 15:9-11

24 Thursday

To give, it is necessary to be free from selfishness.
—Blessed Teresa of Calcutta

25 Friday
Saint Mark, Evangelist
- 1 Pt 5:5b-14 • Ps 89:2-3, 6-7, 16-17 • Mk 16:15-20

26 Saturday
- Acts 16:1-10 • Ps 100:1b-3, 5 • Jn 15:18-21

April

God is a spring of living water that flows unceasingly into the hearts of those who pray.
—St. Louis Mary de Montfort

Sixth Sunday of Easter
- Acts 8:5-8, 14-17 • Ps 66:1-7, 16, 20
- 1 Pt 3:15-18 • Jn 14:15-21

27 Sunday

Saint Peter Chanel;
Saint Louis Mary de Montfort
- Acts 16:11-15 • Ps 149:1b-6a, 9b • Jn 15:26–16:4a

28 Monday

What could move you, God, to such mercy? . . . Only love!
—St. Catherine of Siena

29 Tuesday
Saint Catherine of Siena
- Acts 16:22-34 • Ps 138:1-3, 7c-8 • Jn 16:5-11

30 Wednesday
Pope Saint Pius V
- Acts 17:15, 22–18:1 • Ps 148:1-2, 11-14 • Jn 16:12-15

April

Charity is the form, mover, mother, root of all the virtues.
—St. Thomas Aquinas

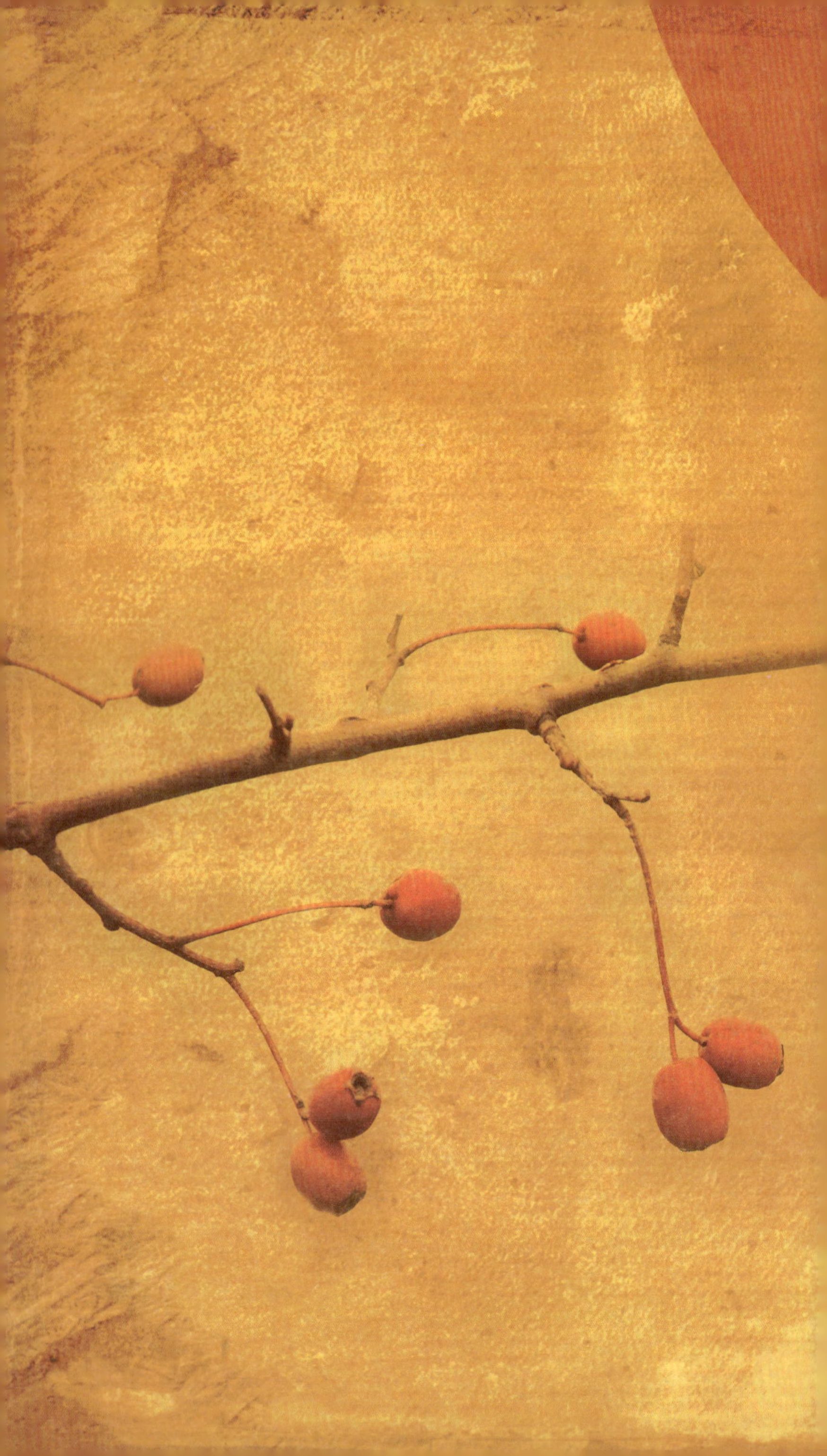

May

[Jesus said:] "I am the true vine and my Father is the vinedresser. Every branch of mine that bears no fruit, he takes away, and every branch that does bear fruit he prunes, that it may bear more fruit. . . . Abide in me, and I in you. As the branch cannot bear fruit by itself, unless it abides in the vine, neither can you, unless you abide in me. I am the vine, you are the branches. He who abides in me, and I in him, he it is that bears much fruit, for apart from me you can do nothing."

—John 15:1-2, 4-5

Today our Lord Jesus Christ ascended into heaven; let our hearts ascend with him. . . . Although he ascended alone, we also ascend, because we are in him by grace.
—St. Augustine

1 Thursday
Acts 18:1-8 • Ps 98:1-4 • Jn 16:16-20
(Ascension: See Sunday, May 4)

2 Friday
Saint Athanasius
• Acts 18:9-18 • Ps 47:2-7 • Jn 16:20-23

Philip said to [Jesus], "Lord, show us the Father, and we shall be satisfied."
—John 14:18

Saint Philip and Saint James, Apostles
- 1 Cor 15:1-8 • Ps 19:2-5 • Jn 14:6-14

3 Saturday

The Ascension of the Lord
- Acts 1:1-11 • Ps 47:2-3, 6-9 • Eph 1:17-23 • Mt 28:16-20

Seventh Sunday of Easter
- Acts 1:12-14 • Ps 27:1, 4, 7-8 • 1 Pt 4:13-16 • Jn 17:1-11a

4 Sunday

MAY

A sincere act of repentance is always the occasion of a new encounter with Our Lord. . . . Heaven is full of great sinners who decided to repent.
—Francis Fernandez

5 Monday
• Acts 19:1-8 • Ps 68:2-7b • Jn 16:29-33

6 Tuesday
• Acts 20:17-27 • Ps 68:10-11, 20-21 • Jn 17:1-11a

> *Love one another in imitation of the union and life of the Lord.*
> —St. Louise de Marillac

• Acts 20:28-38 • Ps 68:29-30, 33-36b • Jn 17:11b-19

7 Wednesday

• Acts 22:30; 23:6-11 • Ps 16:1-2a, 5, 7-11 • Jn 17:20-26

8 Thursday

MAY

Remember always that God is eternal. Work courageously in order one day to be united to him.
—Blessed Damien Joseph de Veuster of Moloka'i

9 Friday
- Acts 25:13b-21 • Ps 103:1-2, 11-12, 19-20b • Jn 21:15-19

10 Saturday
Blessed Damien Joseph de Veuster of Moloka'i
- Acts 28:16-20, 30-31 • Ps 11:4-5, 7 • Jn 21:20-25

Come, Holy Spirit, fill the hearts of all believers and set them on fire with your love.
—Pentecost Antiphon

Pentecost Sunday
- Acts 2:1-11 • Ps 104:1, 24, 29-31, 34
- 1 Cor 12:3b-7, 12-13 • Jn 20:19-23

11 Sunday

Saint Nereus and Saint Achilleus; Saint Pancras
- Jas 1:1-11 • Ps 119:67-68, 71-72, 75-76 • Mk 8:11-13

12 Monday

May

Mary, our heavenly Mother, came to . . . call men to conversion from sin and to spiritual fervor, to inflame souls with love for God and with charity towards their neighbor.
—Pope John Paul II

13 Tuesday
Our Lady of Fatima
- Jas 1:12-18 • Ps 94:12-15, 18-19 • Mk 8:14-21

14 Wednesday
Saint Matthias, Apostle
- Acts 1:15-17, 20-26 • Ps 113:1-8 • Jn 15:9-17

I will bless the Lord at all times; his praise shall continually be in my mouth.

—Psalm 34:1

Saint Isidore
• Jas 2:1-9 • Ps 34:2-7 • Mk 8:27-33

15 THURSDAY

• Jas 2:14-24, 26 • Ps 112:1-6 • Mk 8:34–9:1

16 FRIDAY

MAY

> *You, O eternal Trinity, are a deep ocean,*
> *into which the more I penetrate, the more I discover,*
> *and the more I discover, the more I seek you.*
> —St. Catherine of Siena

17 Saturday
- Jas 3:1-10 • Ps 12:2-5, 7-8 • Mk 9:2-13

18 Sunday
The Most Holy Trinity
- Ex 34:4b-6, 8-9 • (Ps) Dn 3:52-56
- 2 Cor 13:11-13 • Jn 3:16-18

> *If you want to be loved by God, love him
> and he will prosper you. And if you fear him,
> he will protect you from every danger.*
> —St. Bernardine of Siena

• Jas 3:13-18 • Ps 19:8-10, 15 • Mk 9:14-29

19 Monday

Saint Bernardine of Siena
• Jas 4:1-10 • Ps 55:7-11a, 23 • Mk 9:30-37

20 Tuesday

MAY

What is the message that St. Rita of Cascia passes on to us? It is a message that flows from her life: humility and obedience were the path that Rita took to be ever more perfectly conformed to the Crucified One. —Pope John Paul II

21 Wednesday
Saint Christopher Magallanes and Companions
- Jas 4:13-17 • Ps 49:2-3, 6-11 • Mk 9:38-40

22 Thursday
Saint Rita of Cascia
- Jas 5:1-6 • Ps 49:14-20 • Mk 9:41-50

Bless the Lord, O my soul; and all that is within me, bless his holy name.

—Psalm 103:1

• Jas 5:9-12 • Ps 103:1-4, 8-9, 11-12 • Mk 10:1-12

23 Friday

• Jas 5:13-20 • Ps 141:1-3, 8 • Mk 10:13-16

24 Saturday

MAY

*Lord, you are the true nourishment of the soul,
and he who worthily receives you will be partaker
and heir of eternal glory.*

—Thomas à Kempis

25 SUNDAY — The Most Holy Body and Blood of Christ
- Dt 8:2-3, 14b-16a • Ps 147:12-15, 19-20
- 1 Cor 10:16-17 • Jn 6:51-58

26 MONDAY — Saint Philip Neri
- 1 Pt 1:3-9 • Ps 111:1-2, 5-6, 9-10 • Mk 10:17-27

Set your hope fully upon the grace that is coming to you at the revelation of Jesus Christ.

—1 Peter 1:13

Saint Augustine of Canterbury
- 1 Pt 1:10-16 • Ps 98:1-4 • Mk 10:28-31

27 Tuesday

- 1 Pt 1:18-25 • Ps 147:12-15, 19-20 • Mk 10:32-45

28 Wednesday

May

*The human heart of Jesus burns with . . .
love for the eternal Father and for men—the Father's adopted
sons and daughters.*
—Pope John Paul II

29 Thursday
- 1 Pt 2:2-5, 9-12 • Ps 100:2-5 • Mk 10:46-52

30 Friday
The Most Sacred Heart of Jesus
- Dt 7:6-11 • Ps 103:1-4, 6-8, 10 • 1 Jn 4:7-16 • Mt 11:25-30

Let the soul of Mary be in each of us to magnify the Lord, and the spirit of Mary be in each of us to rejoice in God.
—St. Anselm

The Visitation of the Blessed Virgin Mary
• Zep 3:14-18a or Rom 12:9-16 • (Ps) Is 12:2-6 • Lk 1:39-56

31 SATURDAY

MAY

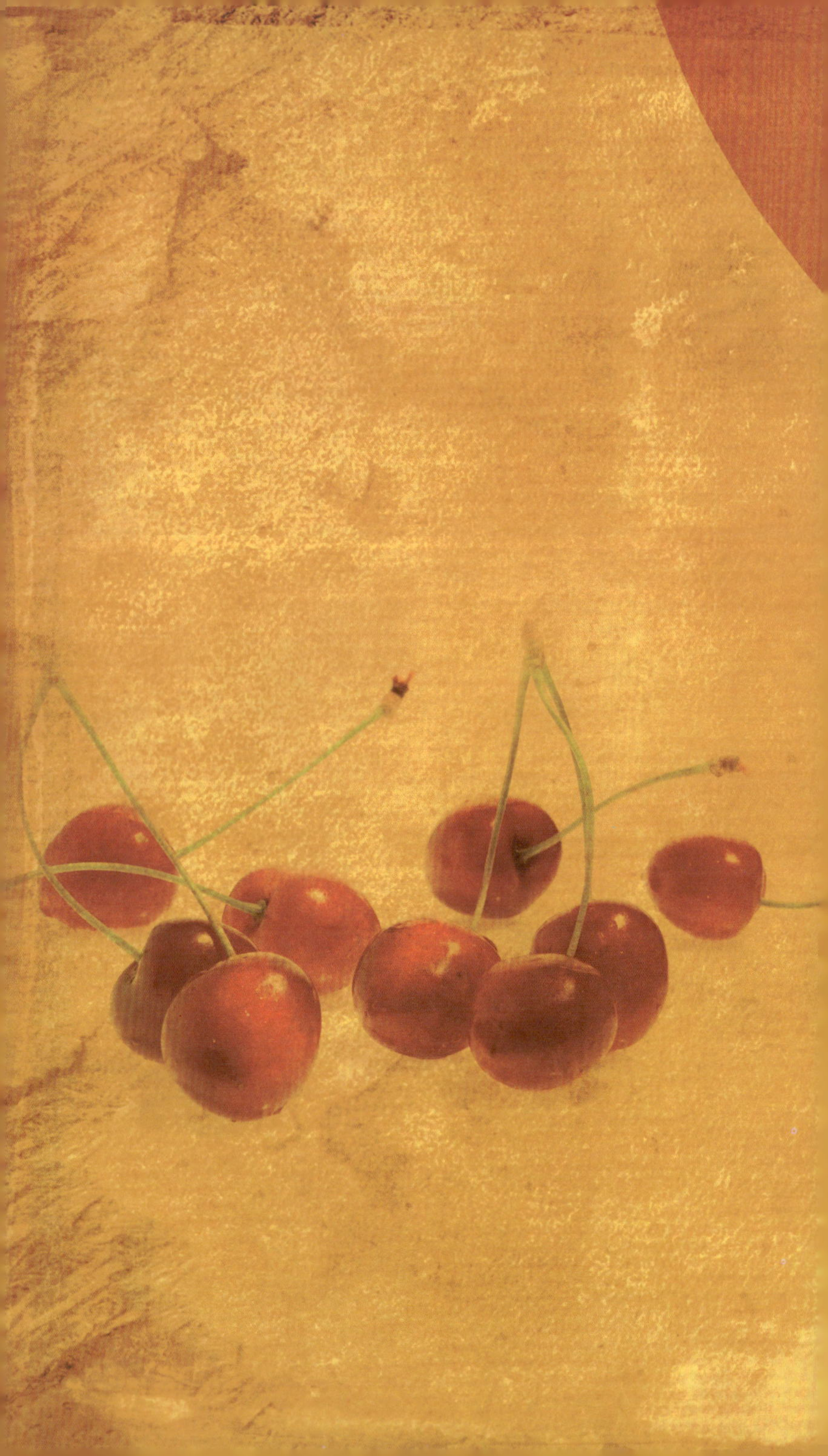

June

*Love is a fruit that is in season at all times
and within the reach of every hand.
Anyone may gather it and no limit is set.
Everyone can reach this love through meditation,
spirit of prayer, and sacrifice, by an intense inner life.*

—Blessed Teresa of Calcutta

We should love God because he is God, and the measure of our love should be to love him without measure.
—St. Bernard of Clairvaux

1 Sunday
Ninth Sunday in Ordinary Time
- Dt 11:18, 26-28, 32 • Ps 31:2-4, 17, 25
- Rom 3:21-25, 28 • Mt 7:21-27

2 Monday
Saint Marcellinus and Saint Peter
- 2 Pt 1:2-7 • Ps 91:1-2, 14-16 • Mk 12:1-12

JUNE

The death of the martyrs blossoms in the faith of the living.
—Pope St. Gregory the Great

Saint Charles Lwanga and Companions
• 2 Pt 3:12-15a, 17-18 • Ps 90:2-4, 10, 14, 16 • Mk 12:13-17

3 Tuesday

• 2 Tm 1:1-3, 6-12 • Ps 123:1b-2 • Mk 12:18-27

4 Wednesday

What we ourselves cannot bear let us bear with the help of Christ. For he tells us: My yoke is easy and my burden is light.
—St. Boniface

5 Thursday

Saint Boniface
- 2 Tm 2:8-15 • Ps 25:4-5b, 8-10, 14 • Mk 12:28-34

6 Friday

Saint Norbert
- 2 Tm 3:10-17 • Ps 119:157, 160-161, 165-166, 168
- Mk 12:35-37

JUNE

Let us know, let us press on to know the LORD.
—HOSEA 6:3

• 2 Tm 4:1-8 • Ps 71:8-9, 14-17, 22 • Mk 12:38-44

7
SATURDAY

TENTH SUNDAY IN ORDINARY TIME
• Hos 6:3-6 • Ps 50:1, 8, 12-15 • Rom 4:18-25 • Mt 9:9-13

8
SUNDAY

*If you pray before you work, the passageway
into the soul will not be open to sin.*

—St. Ephrem

9
Monday

Saint Ephrem
- 1 Kgs 17:1-6 • Ps 121:1-8 • Mt 5:1-12

10
Tuesday

- 1 Kgs 17:7-16 • Ps 4:2-5, 7b-8 • Mt 5:13-16

June

> *You shall love him who made you . . . you shall glorify him who redeemed you from death. You shall be simple in heart and rich in spirit.*
>
> —Epistle of Barnabas

Saint Barnabas, Apostle
- Acts 11:21b-26; 13:1-3 • Ps 98:1-6 • Mt 5:17-19

11 Wednesday

- 1 Kgs 18:41-46 • Ps 65:10-13 • Mt 5:20-26

12 Thursday

Nothing apart from God can satisfy the human heart that is truly in search of him.

—St. Anthony of Padua

13 Friday

Saint Anthony of Padua
- 1 Kgs 19:9a, 11-16 • Ps 27:7-9, 13-14 • Mt 5:27-32

14 Saturday
- 1 Kgs 19:19-21 • Ps 16:1b-2a, 5, 7-10 • Mt 5:33-37

June

> *Worship the Lord with gladness;*
> *come into his presence with singing.*
> —Psalm 100:2

Eleventh Sunday in Ordinary Time
• Ex 19:2-6a • Ps 100:1-3, 5 • Rom 5:6-11 • Mt 9:36–10:8

15 Sunday

• 1 Kgs 21:1-16 • Ps 5:2-7 • Mt 5:38-42

16 Monday

Hope not in yourself but in God.
—St. Augustine

17
Tuesday
- 1 Kgs 21:17-29 • Ps 51:3b, 11, 16 • Mt 5:43-48

18
Wednesday
- 2 Kgs 2:1, 6-14 • Ps 31:20-21, 24 • Mt 6:1-6, 16-18

June

*Beloved Jesus, beloved, sweet honey, indescribable longing,
delight of the saints, sweetness of the angels!*
—St. Romuald

Saint Romuald
• Sir 48:1-14 • Ps 97:1-7 • Mt 6:7-15

19
Thursday

• 2 Kgs 11:1-4, 9-20 • Ps 132:11-14, 17-18 • Mt 6:19-23

20
Friday

Of what use are riches in eternity?
—St. Aloysius Gonzaga

21 Saturday — Saint Aloysius Gonzaga
- 2 Chr 24:17-25 • Ps 89:4-5, 29-34 • Mt 6:24-34

22 Sunday — Twelfth Sunday in Ordinary Time
- Jer 20:10-13 • Ps 69:8-10, 14, 17, 33-35
- Rom 5:12-15 • Mt 10:26-33

June

"He must increase, but I must decrease" (John 3:30): the Baptist's words are a program for every Christian.
—Pope Benedict XVI

• 2 Kgs 17:5-8, 13-15a, 18 • Ps 60:3-5, 12-13 • Mt 7:1-5

23 Monday

The Nativity of Saint John the Baptist
• Is 49:1-6 • Ps 139:1b-3, 13-15 • Acts 13:22-26 • Lk 1:57-66, 80

24 Tuesday

*Lead me in the path of your commandments,
for I delight in it.*
—Psalm 119:35

25 WEDNESDAY • 2 Kgs 22:8-13; 23:1-3 • Ps 119:33-37, 40 • Mt 7:15-20

26 THURSDAY • 2 Kgs 24:8-17 • Ps 79:1b-5, 8-9 • Mt 7:21-29

JUNE

God did not make the first man because he needed company, but because he wanted someone to whom he could show his generosity and love.

—St. Irenaeus

Saint Cyril of Alexandria
- 2 Kgs 25:1-12 • Ps 137:1-6 • Mt 8:1-4

27 Friday

Saint Irenaeus
- Lam 2:2, 10-14, 18-19 • Ps 74:1b-7, 20-21 • Mt 8:5-17

28 Saturday

The blood of martyrs is the seed of Christians.
—Tertullian

29 Sunday
Saint Peter and Saint Paul, Apostles
- Acts 12:1-11 • Ps 34:2-9 • 2 Tm 4:6-8, 17-18 • Mt 16:13-19

30 Monday
The First Martyrs of the Roman Church
- Am 2:6-10, 13-16 • Ps 50:16b-23 • Mt 8:18-22

JUNE

It is in pardoning that we are pardoned.
—St. Francis of Assisi

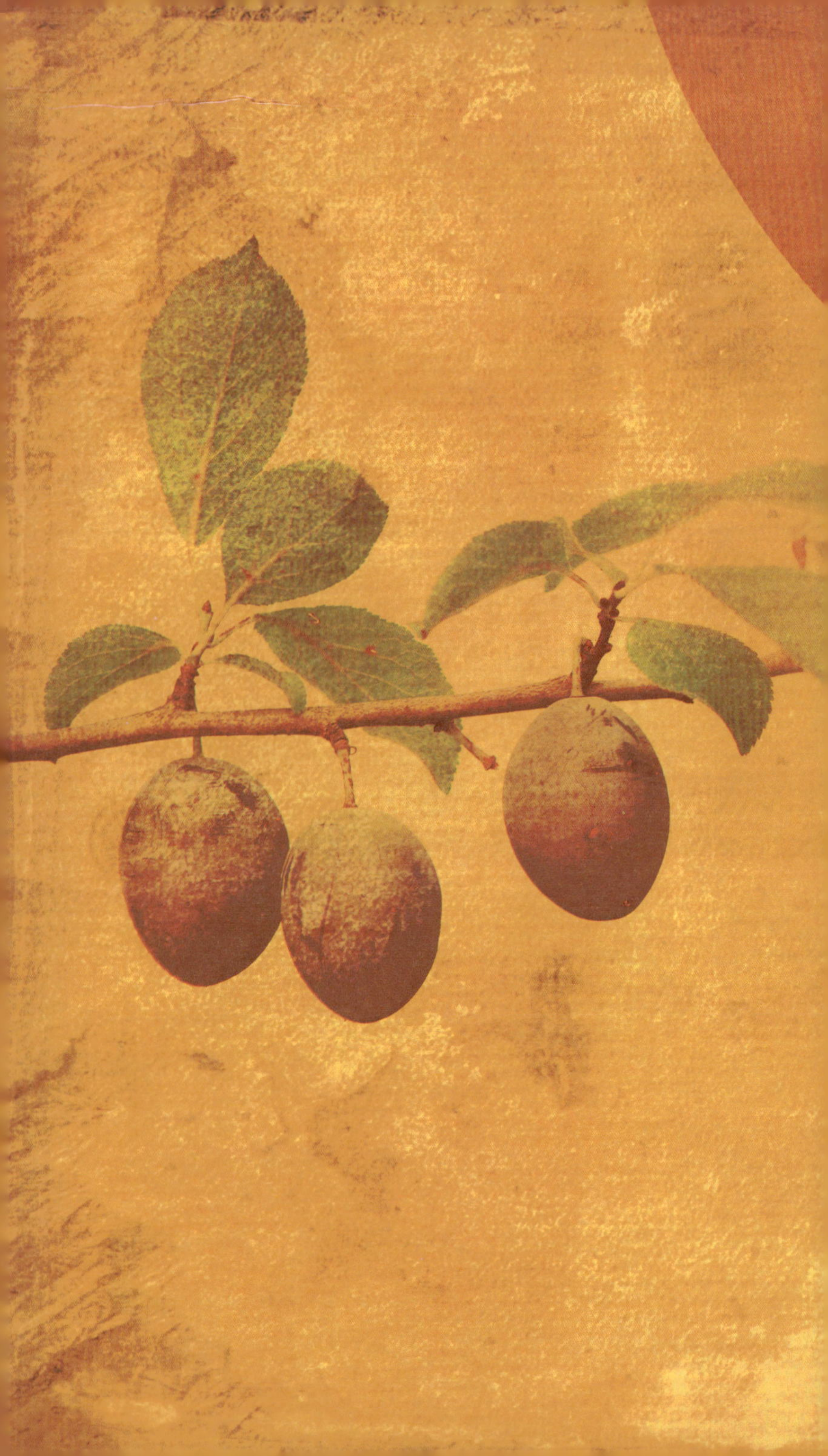

July

Those blessed fruits enumerated by the apostle, the Spirit produces and shows forth in the just, even in this mortal life—fruits replete with all sweetness and joy. Such must, indeed, be from the Spirit "who in the Trinity is the love of the Father and the Son, filling all creatures with immeasurable sweetness" [St. Augustine].

—Pope Leo XIII

Of all things of life, a happy death is our principal concern. For if we attain that, it matters little if we lose all the rest. But if we do not attain that, nothing else is of any value.

—Blessed Junípero Serra

1 Tuesday

Blessed Junípero Serra
- Am 3:1-8; 4:11-12 • Ps 5:4b-8 • Mt 8:23-27

2 Wednesday

- Am 5:14-15, 21-24 • Ps 50:7-13, 16b-17 • Mt 8:28-34

Jesus said to [Thomas], "Have you believed because you have seen me? Blessed are those who have not seen and yet believe."
—John 20:29

Saint Thomas, Apostle
- Eph 2:19-22 • Ps 117:1b-2 • Jn 20:24-29

3 Thursday

Saint Elizabeth of Portugal; Independence Day
- Am 8:4-6, 9-12 • Ps 119:2, 10, 20, 30, 40, 131 • Mt 9:9-13

4 Friday

July

> *We should love and feel compassion for those who oppose us, since they harm themselves and do us good, and adorn us with crowns of everlasting glory.*
> —St. Anthony Mary Zaccaria

5 Saturday
Saint Anthony Mary Zaccaria
- Am 9:11-15 • Ps 85:9-14 • Mt 9:14-17

6 Sunday
Fourteenth Sunday in Ordinary Time
- Zec 9:9-10 • Ps 145:1-2, 8-11, 13-14 • Rom 8:9, 11-13
- Mt 11:25-30

The Lord is gracious and merciful, slow to anger and abounding in steadfast love.
—Psalm 145:8

• Hos 2:16, 17b-18, 21-22 • Ps 145:2-9 • Mt 9:18-26

7
Monday

• Hos 8:4-7, 11-13 • Ps 115:3-10 • Mt 9:32-38

8
Tuesday

JULY

Every piece of my flesh, every drop of my blood will tell you that I am Christian.

—St. Chi Zhuzi, Companion of St. Augustine Zhao Rong

9 Wednesday

Saint Augustine Zhao Rong and Companions
- Hos 10:1-3, 7-8, 12 • Ps 105:2-7 • Mt 10:1-7

10 Thursday

- Hos 11:1-4, 8c-9 • Ps 80:2-3b, 15-16 • Mt 10:7-15

Girded with faith and the performance of good deeds, let us follow in his paths by the guidance of the gospel; then we shall deserve to see him who has called us into his kingdom.
—Rule of St. Benedict

Saint Benedict
• Hos 14:2-10 • Ps 51:3-4, 8-9, 12-14, 17 • Mt 10:16-23

11 Friday

• Is 6:1-8 • Ps 93:1-2, 5 • Mt 10:24-33

12 Saturday

July

Jesus, Mary, I love you.
—Blessed Kateri Tekakwitha's
Last Words on Her Deathbed

13 Sunday
Fifteenth Sunday in Ordinary Time
- Is 55:10-11 • Ps 65:10-14 • Rom 8:18-23 • Mt 13:1-23

14 Monday
Blessed Kateri Tekakwitha
- Is 1:10-17 • Ps 50:8-9, 16b-17, 21, 23 • Mt 10:34–11:1

When we pray, the voice of the heart must be heard more than the proceedings from the mouth.
—St. Bonaventure

Saint Bonaventure
• Is 7:1-9 • Ps 48:2-8 • Mt 11:20-24

15
Tuesday

Our Lady of Mount Carmel
• Is 10:5-7, 13b-16 • Ps 94:5-10, 14-15 • Mt 11:25-27

16
Wednesday

JULY

Think well. Speak well. Do well. These three things, through the mercy of God, will make a man go to heaven.
—St. Camillus de Lellis

17
Thursday
• Is 26:7-9, 12, 16-19 • Ps 102:13-21 • Mt 11:28-30

18
Friday
Saint Camillus de Lellis
• Is 38:1-8, 21-22 • (Ps) Is 38:10-12, 16 • Mt 12:1-8

> *We do not know how to pray as we ought, but the Spirit himself intercedes for us with sighs too deep for words.*
> —Romans 8:26

• Mi 2:1-5 • Ps 10:1-4, 7-8, 14 • Mt 12:14-21

19 Saturday

Sixteenth Sunday in Ordinary Time
• Wis 12:13, 16-19 • Ps 86:5-6, 9-10, 15-16
• Rom 8:26-27 • Mt 13:24-43

20 Sunday

JULY

*The Magdalene, most of all, is the model I like to follow.
That boldness of hers—the boldness of a lover—won the heart
of Jesus, and how it fascinates mine!*
—St. Thérèse of Lisieux

21 Monday
Saint Lawrence of Brindisi
• Mi 6:1-4, 6-8 • Ps 50:5-6, 8-9, 16b-17, 21, 23 • Mt 12:38-42

22 Tuesday
Saint Mary Magdalene
• Mi 7:14-15, 18-20 • Ps 85:2-8 • Jn 20:1-2, 11-18

> *My mercy is that none of my enemies is so thorough or so great a sinner that I would deny him my forgiveness if he were to ask for it.*
> —Christ's Revelation to St. Bridget

Saint Bridget of Sweden
• Jer 1:1, 4-10 • Ps 71:1-6b, 15, 17 • Mt 13:1-9

23
Wednesday

Saint Sharbel Makhluf
• Jer 2:1-3, 7-8, 12-13 • Ps 36:6-11 • Mt 13:10-17

24
Thursday

JULY

Today we ask Saints Joachim and Anne to help us make our Christian homes places where God can easily be found.
—Francis Fernandez

25 Friday
Saint James, Apostle
- 2 Cor 4:7-15 • Ps 126:1-6 • Mt 20:20-28

26 Saturday
Saint Joachim and Saint Anne, Parents of Mary
- Jer 7:1-11 • Ps 84:3-6a, 8a, 11 • Mt 13:24-30

*The unfolding of your words gives light;
it imparts understanding to the simple.*

—PSALM 119:130

Seventeenth Sunday in Ordinary Time
- 1 Kgs 3:5, 7-12 • Ps 119:57, 72, 76-77, 127-130
- Rom 8:28-30 • Mt 13:44-52

27 Sunday

- Jer 13:1-11 • (Ps) Dt 32:18-21 • Mt 13:31-35

28 Monday

JULY

> *Martha welcomes Jesus in . . . [her hospitality] is human warmth offering to supply for human need in another, in this case Jesus, presenting himself to her in his humble, human necessity.* —CARDINAL ANASTASIO BALLESTRERO

29 TUESDAY
SAINT MARTHA
- Jer 14:17-22 • Ps 32:18-21 • Jn 11:19-27 or Lk 10:38-42

30 WEDNESDAY
SAINT PETER CHRYSOLOGUS
- Jer 15:10, 16-21 • Ps 59:2-4, 10-11, 17-18 • Mt 13:44-46

> *Every fresh Communion is a new gift that Jesus Christ makes of himself.*
> —St. Ignatius of Loyola

Saint Ignatius of Loyola
- Jer 18:1-6 • Ps 146:1b-6b • Mt 13:47-53

31 Thursday

JULY

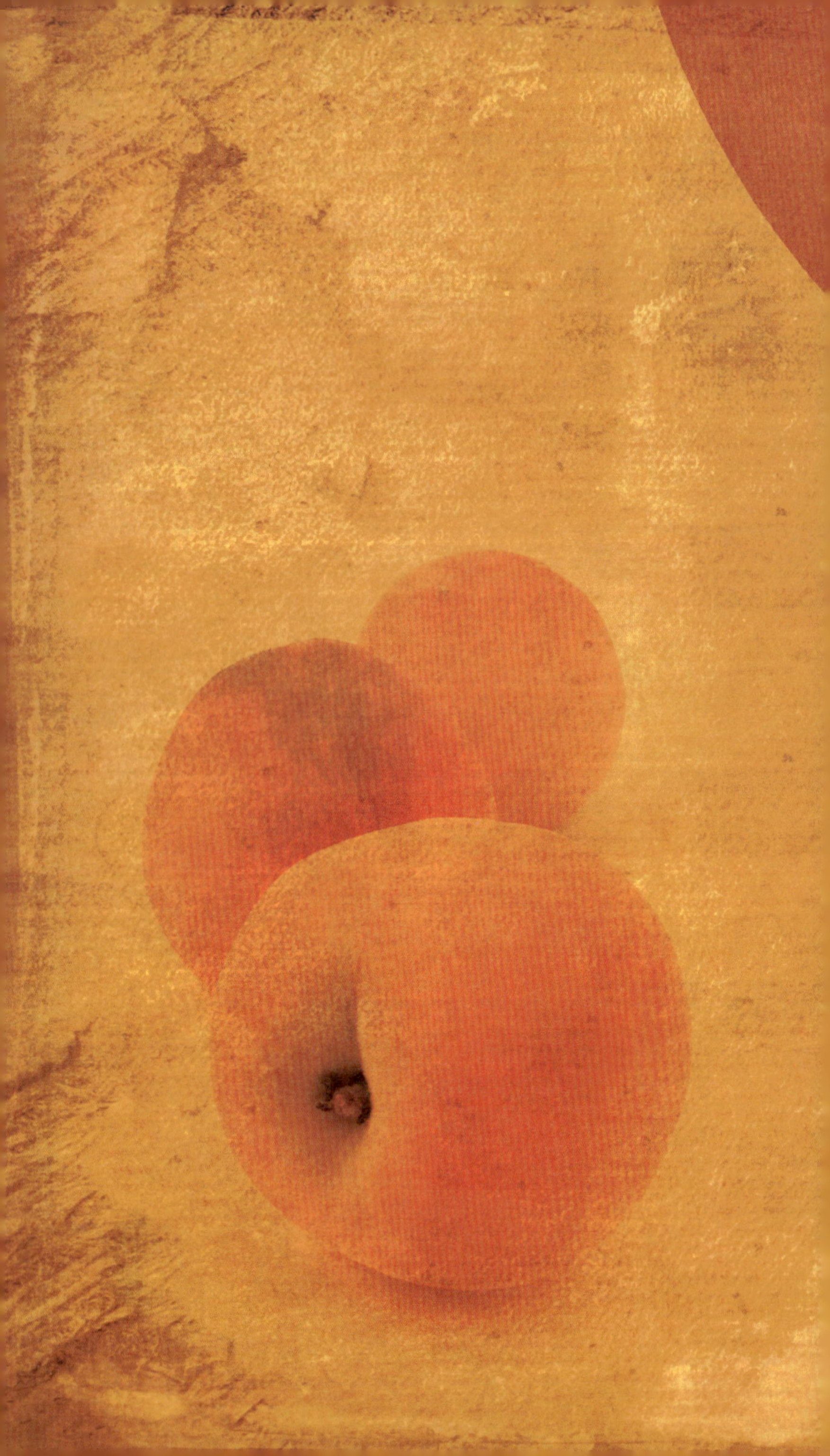

AUGUST

When you are excited to impatience, think for a moment how much more reason God has to be angry with you, than you can have for anger against any human being; and yet how constant is his patience and forbearance.

—St. Elizabeth Ann Seton

We have only one evil to fear, and that is sin.
—St. Alphonsus Liguori

1 Friday
Saint Alphonsus Liguori
• Jer 26:1-9 • Ps 69:5, 8-10, 14 • Mt 13:54-58

2 Saturday
Saint Eusebius of Vercelli;
Saint Peter Julian Eymard
• Jer 26:11-16, 24 • Ps 69:15-16, 30-31, 33-34 • Mt 14:1-12

August

> *To approach God, one should go straight to him, like a ball from a cannon.*
> —St. John Mary Vianney

Eighteenth Sunday in Ordinary Time
• Is 55:1-3 • Ps 145:8-9, 15-18 • Rom 8:35, 37-39 • Mt 14:13-21

3 Sunday

Saint John Mary Vianney
• Jer 28:1-17 • Ps 119:29, 43, 79-80, 95, 102 • Mt 14:22-36

4 Monday

> *[Jesus'] glory shone from a body like our own,*
> *to show that the church which is the body of Christ*
> *would one day share his glory.*
>
> —Preface, Mass for the Feast of the Transfiguration

5 Tuesday
The Dedication of the Basilica of Saint Mary Major in Rome
- Jer 30:1-2, 12-15, 18-22 • Ps 102:16-23, 29
- Mt 14:22-36 or 15:1-2, 10-14

6 Wednesday
The Transfiguration of the Lord
- Dn 7:9-10, 13-14 • Ps 97:1-2, 5-6, 9 • 2 Pt 1:16-19 • Mt 17:1-9

August

> *One who governs his passions is master of the world.*
> *We must either command them, or be commanded by them.*
> —St. Dominic

Pope Saint Sixtus II and Companions; Saint Cajetan
• Jer 31:31-34 • Ps 51:12-15, 18-19 • Mt 16:13-23

7 Thursday

Saint Dominic
• Na 2:1, 3; 3:1-3, 6-7 • (Ps) Dt 32:35c-36b, 39, 41 • Mt 16:24-28

8 Friday

If anyone comes to me, I want to lead them to Jesus.
—St. Teresa Benedicta of the Cross (Edith Stein)

9 Saturday
Saint Teresa Benedicta of the Cross (Edith Stein)
- Hb 1:12–2:4 • Ps 9:8-13 • Mt 17:14-20

10 Sunday
Nineteenth Sunday in Ordinary Time
- 1 Kgs 19:9a, 11-13a • Ps 85:9-14 • Rom 9:1-5 • Mt 14:22-33

AUGUST

Our labor here is brief, but the reward is eternal.
—St. Clare of Assisi

Saint Clare
- Ez 1:2-5, 24-28c • Ps 148:1-2, 11-14 • Mt 17:22-27

11 Monday

- Ez 2:8–3:4 • Ps 119:14, 24, 72, 103, 111, 131
- Mt 18:1-5, 10, 12-14

12 Tuesday

Jesus Christ is our sublime guide toward growth in God's love.

—St. Maximilian Mary Kolbe

13 WEDNESDAY
Pope Saint Pontian and Saint Hippolytus
- Ez 9:1-7; 10:18-22 • Ps 113:1-6 • Mt 18:15-20

14 THURSDAY
Saint Maximilian Mary Kolbe
- Ez 12:1-12 • Ps 78:56-59, 61-62 • Mt 18:21–19:1

AUGUST

> *The assumption of the Blessed Virgin is a singular participation in her Son's resurrection and an anticipation of the resurrection of other Christians.*
> —CATECHISM OF THE CATHOLIC CHURCH, 966

THE ASSUMPTION OF THE BLESSED VIRGIN MARY
HOLY DAY OF OBLGATION
- Rv 11:19a; 12:1-6a, 10ab • Ps 45:10-12, 16
- 1 Cor 15:20-27 • Lk 1:39-56

15 FRIDAY

SAINT STEPHEN OF HUNGARY
- Ez 18:1-10, 13b, 30-32 • Ps 51:12-15, 18-19 • Mt 19:13-15

16 SATURDAY

Surrender yourself completely to the care and the everlasting love God has for you.
—St. Jane Frances de Chantal

17 Sunday
Twentieth Sunday in Ordinary Time
- Is 56:1, 6-7 • Ps 67:2-3, 5-6, 8 • Rom 11:13-15, 29-32
- Mt 15:21-28

18 Monday
Saint Jane Frances de Chantal
- Ez 24:15-24 • (Ps) Dt 32:18-21 • Mt 19:16-22

August

Jesus is my all, and I desire to belong wholly to him. It is extreme folly and delusion to look elsewhere for any true happiness.
—St. John Eudes

Saint John Eudes
- Ez 28:1-10 • (Ps) Dt 32:26-28, 30, 35c-36b • Mt 19:23-30

19 Tuesday

Saint Bernard
- Ez 34:1-11 • Ps 23:1-6 • Mt 20:1-16

20 Wednesday

> *Our Queen is constantly before the Divine Majesty, interceding for us with her most powerful prayers.*
> —Blessed Amadeus

21 Thursday
Pope Saint Pius X
- Ez 36:23-28 • Ps 51:12-15, 18-19 • Mt 22:1-14

22 Friday
The Queenship of the Blessed Virgin Mary
- Ez 37:1-14 • Ps 107:2-9 • Mt 22:34-40

August

When we serve the poor and the sick, we serve Jesus. We must not fail to help our neighbors, because in them we serve Jesus.
—St. Rose of Lima

Saint Rose of Lima
- Ez 43:1-7ab • Ps 85:9-14 • Mt 23:1-12

23 Saturday

Twenty-first Sunday in Ordinary Time
- Is 22:19-23 • Ps 138:1-3, 6, 8 • Rom 11:33-36 • Mt 16:13-20

24 Sunday

> *May the Lord give you the grace to do his will,
> so that he may be served and honored through you.*
> —St. Louis of France

25
Monday

SAINT LOUIS OF FRANCE; SAINT JOSEPH CALASANZ
• 2 Th 1:1-5, 11-12 • Ps 96:1-5 • Mt 23:13-22

26
Tuesday

• 2 Th 2:1-3a, 14-17 • Ps 96:10-13 • Mt 23:23-26

AUGUST

Patience is the companion of wisdom.
—St. Augustine

Saint Monica
• 2 Th 3:6-10, 16-18 • Ps 128:1-2, 4-5 • Mt 23:27-32

27 WEDNESDAY

Saint Augustine
• 1 Cor 1:1-9 • Ps 145:2-7 • Mt 24:42-51

28 THURSDAY

Look today to John the Baptist, an enduring model of fidelity to God and his law. . . . Imitate him with docile and trusting generosity.
—Pope John Paul II

29 Friday
The Martyrdom of Saint John the Baptist
- 1 Cor 1:17-25 • Ps 33:1-2, 4-5, 10-11 • Mk 6:17-29

30 Saturday
- 1 Cor 1:26-31 • Ps 33:12-13, 18-21 • Mt 25:14-30

AUGUST

O God, you are my God, I seek you, my soul thirsts for you.
—Psalm 63:1

Twenty-second Sunday in Ordinary Time
• Jer 20:7-9 • Ps 63:2-6, 8-9 • Rom 12:1-2 • Mt 16:21-27

31
Sunday

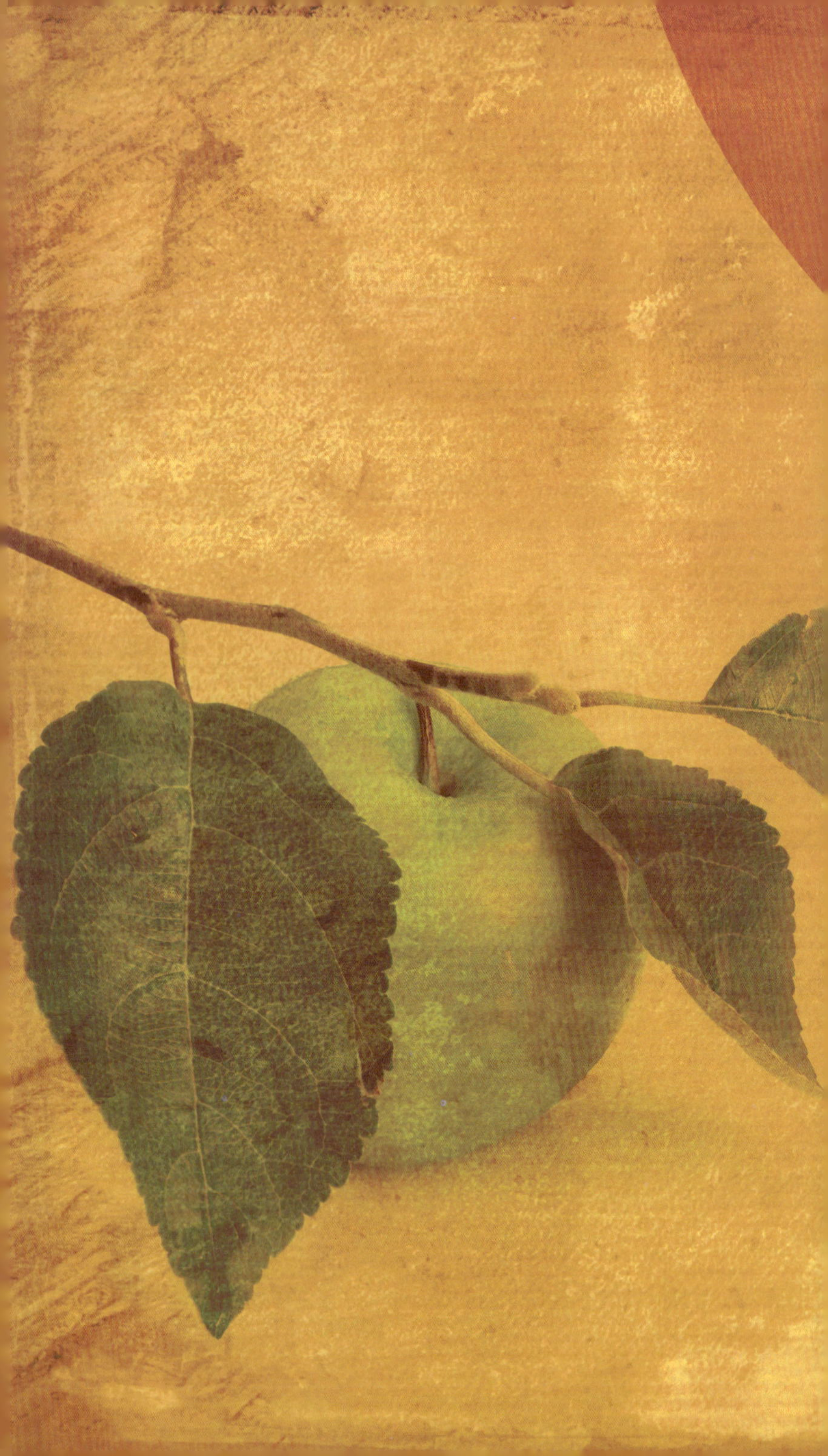

September

*Peace is nourished from the rich fruifulness of charity.
It is the nursling daughter of faith, the supporting column
of justice. Peace is a suitable pledge of future hope.
Peace, which unites those present, invites the absent.
This peace reconciles earthly things with the heavenly
and human matters with the divine.*

—St. Peter Chrysologus

He who does not abide in his littleness loses his greatness.
—St. Francis de Sales

1
Monday

Labor Day
• 1 Cor 2:1-5 • Ps 119:97-102 • Lk 4:16-30

2
Tuesday

• 1 Cor 2:10b-16 • Ps 145:8-14 • Lk 4:31-37

Patience is the root and guardian of all the virtues.
—Pope St. Gregory the Great

Pope Saint Gregory the Great
- 1 Cor 3:1-9 • Ps 33:12-15, 20-21 • Lk 4:38-44

3 Wednesday

- 1 Cor 3:18-23 • Ps 24:1b-6 • Lk 5:1-11

4 Thursday

SEPTEMBER

Commit your way to the Lord; trust in him, and he will act.
—Psalm 37:5

5 Friday
- 1 Cor 4:1-5 • Ps 37:3-6, 27-28, 39-40 • Lk 5:33-39

6 Saturday
- 1 Cor 4:6b-15 • Ps 145:17-21 • Lk 6:1-5

Mary is the sure path to our meeting with Christ.
—Pope John Paul II

Twenty-third Sunday in Ordinary Time
• Ez 33:7-9 • Ps 95:1-2, 6-9 • Rom 13:8-10 • Mt 18:15-20

7 Sunday

The Nativity of the Blessed Virgin Mary
• Mi 5:1-4a or Rom 8:28-30 • Ps 13:6 • Mt 1:1-16, 18-23

8 Monday

SEPTEMBER

Seek God and endeavor to find him in all things.
—St. Peter Claver

9 Tuesday

Saint Peter Claver
- 1 Cor 6:1-11 • Ps 149:1b-6a, 9b • Lk 6:12-19

10 Wednesday
- 1 Cor 7:25-31 • Ps 45:11-12, 14-17 • Lk 6:20-26

> *In danger, in doubts, in difficulties,*
> *think of Mary, call upon Mary. . . .*
> *Don't let her name depart from your lips.*
> —St. Bernard of Clairvaux

• 1 Cor 8:1b-7, 11-13 • Ps 139:1b-3, 13-14b, 23-24 • Lk 6:27-38

11 Thursday

The Most Holy Name of Mary
• 1 Cor 9:16-19, 22b-27 • Ps 84:3-6, 12 • Lk 6:39-42

12 Friday

September

> *Whoever seeks earth before he seeks heaven
> will surely lose both earth and heaven.*
> —St. John Chrysostom

13 Saturday — Saint John Chrysostom
- 1 Cor 10:14-22 • Ps 116:12-13, 17-18 • Lk 6:43-49

14 Sunday — The Exaltation of the Holy Cross
- Nm 21:4b-9 • Ps 78:1b-2, 34-38 • Phil 2:6-11 • Jn 3:13-17

The new man, reborn and restored to his God by grace, says first of all, "Father!" because he has now begun to be a son.
—St. Cyprian

Our Lady of Sorrows
• 1 Cor 11:17-26, 33 • Ps 40:7-10, 17 • Jn 19:25-27 or Lk 2:33-35

15 Monday

Pope Saint Cornelius and Saint Cyprian
• 1 Cor 12:12-14, 27-31a • Ps 100:1b-5 • Lk 7:11-17

16 Tuesday

SEPTEMBER

*Charity is that with which no one is lost,
and without which no one is saved.*
—St. Robert Bellarmine

17 Wednesday

Saint Robert Bellarmine
- 1 Cor 12:31–13:13 • Ps 33:2-5, 12, 22 • Lk 7:31-35

18 Thursday

- 1 Cor 15:1-11 • Ps 118:1b-2, 16b-17, 28 • Lk 7:36-50

Hold fast to the will of God and with all your heart fight the good fight under the leadership of Jesus.

—St. Andrew Kim Taegon

Saint Januarius
- 1 Cor 15:12-20 • Ps 17:1, 6-8b, 15 • Lk 8:1-3

19 Friday

Saint Andrew Kim Taegon, Saint Paul Chong Hasang, and Companions
- 1 Cor 15:35-37, 42-49 • Ps 56:10c-14 • Lk 8:4-15

20 Saturday

SEPTEMBER

The Lord is near to all who call on him.
—Psalm 145:18

21 Sunday
Twenty-fifth Sunday in Ordinary Time
- Is 55:6-9 • Ps 145:2-3, 8-9, 17-18
- Phil 1:20c-24, 27a • Mt 20:1-16a

22 Monday
- Prv 3:27-34 • Ps 15:2-5 • Lk 8:16-18

Do everything for the love of God and his glory without looking at the outcome of the undertaking. Work is judged not by its results, but by its intention.

—St. Pio of Pietrelcina

Saint Pio of Pietrelcina

• Prv 21:1-6, 10-13 • Ps 119:1, 27, 30, 34-35, 44 • Lk 8:19-21

23 Tuesday

• Prv 30:5-9 • Ps 119:29, 72, 89, 101, 104, 163 • Lk 9:1-6

24 Wednesday

September

*Let the favor of the Lord our God be upon us,
and prosper for us the work of our hands.*
—Psalm 90:17

25 Thursday

- Eccl 1:2-11 • Ps 90:3-6, 12-14, 17 • Lk 9:7-9

26 Friday

Saint Cosmas and Saint Damian
- Eccl 3:1-11 • Ps 144:1b-4 • Lk 9:18-22

> *We should have no other object but God in our actions and seek to please him alone in all things.*
> —St. Vincent de Paul

Saint Vincent de Paul
- Eccl 11:9–12:8 • Ps 90:3-6, 12-14, 17 • Lk 9:43b-45

27 Saturday

Twenty-sixth Sunday in Ordinary Time
- Ez 18:25-28 • Ps 25:4-5, 8-10, 14 • Phil 2:1-11 • Mt 21:28-32

28 Sunday

SEPTEMBER

> *In the lives of Christians we look not to the beginnings but to the endings.*
> —St. Jerome

29 MONDAY
Saint Michael, Saint Gabriel, and Saint Raphael, archangels
- Dn 7:9-10, 13-14 or Rv 12:7-12a • Ps 138:1-5 • Jn 1:47-51

30 TUESDAY
Saint Jerome
- Jb 3:1-3, 11-17, 20-23 • Ps 88:2-8 • Lk 9:51-56

With mind entire, faith firm, courage undaunted, love thorough, let us be ready for whatever God wills.
—St. Bede the Venerable

A Reminder

All of us at The Word Among Us hope that this year's "Bearing the Fruit of the Spirit" theme has been inspirational for your prayer and journaling. Since so many people begin selecting calendars and planners at this time, we want to encourage you to reserve your copy of next year's edition now. If you find that The Word Among Us Prayer Journal has added to your prayer and appreciation of Scripture, please make it a point to call toll free this week.

1-800-775-9673

or order online at www.wordamongus.org

Visa, MasterCard, Discover Card accepted.

SEPTEMBER

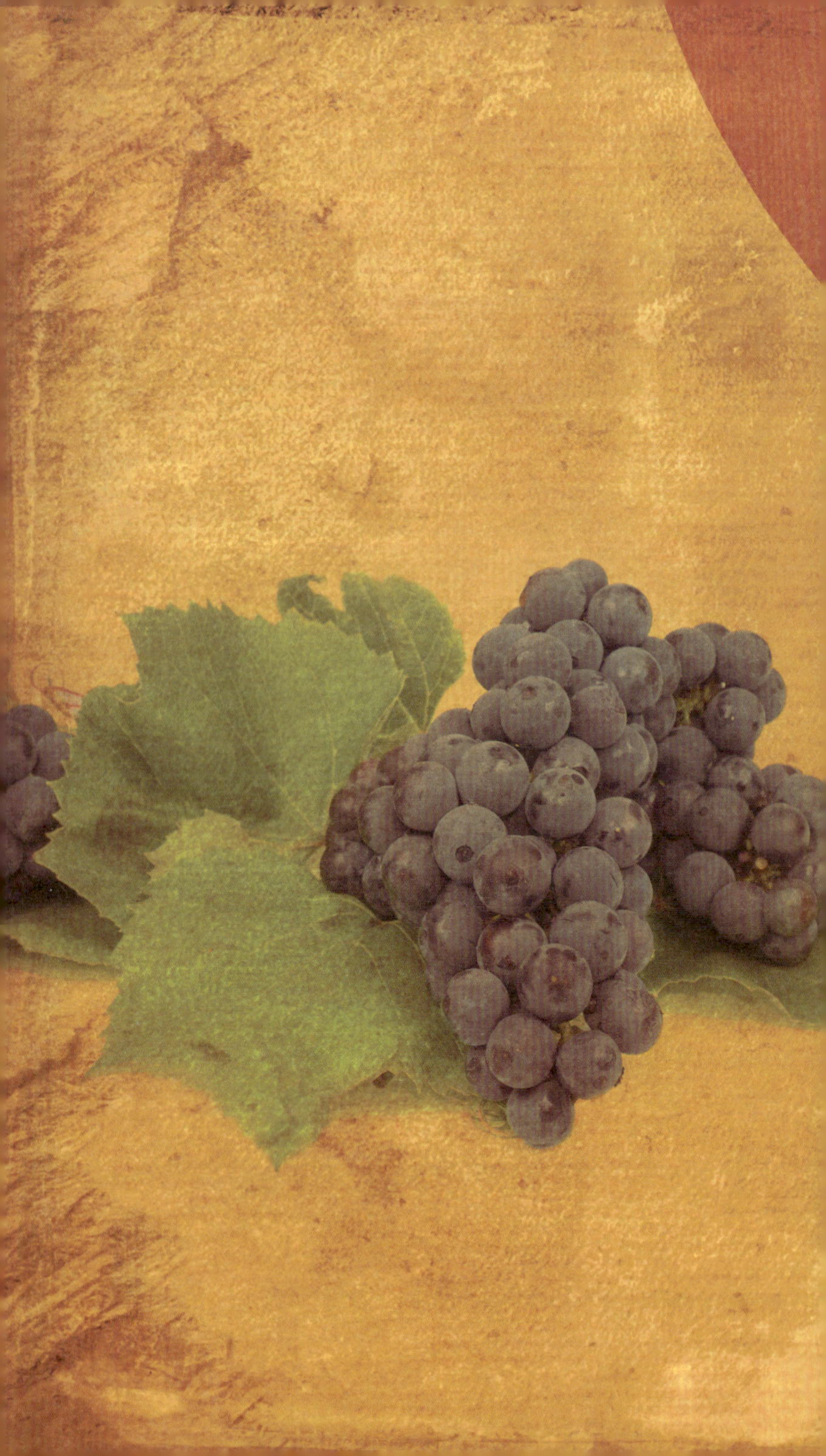

October

When a fruit first comes forth on a plant, it is green, hard, and bitter. Eventually, when the fruit develops to the fullness of its maturity, it becomes sweet and soft. So it is with the fruits of the Holy Spirit. The more we use them, the easier and the sweeter it becomes to exercise them.

—Pope John Paul II, 2003 Pentecost Homily

*I want only one thing: to begin to sing now what
I will sing for all eternity—the mercies of the Lord.*

—St. Thérèse of Lisieux (of the Child Jesus)

1 WEDNESDAY
Saint Thérèse of the Child Jesus
• Jb 9:1-12, 14-16 • Ps 88:10b-15 • Lk 9:57-62

2 THURSDAY
The Guardian Angels
• Jb 19:21-27 • Ps 27:7-9, 13-14 • Mt 18:1-5, 10

OCTOBER

While you are proclaiming peace with your lips, be careful to have it even more fully in your heart.
—St. Francis of Assisi

• Jb 38:1, 12-21; 40:3-5 • Ps 139:1-3, 7-10, 13-14b • Lk 10:13-16

3 Friday

Saint Francis of Assisi
• Jb 42:1-6, 12-17 • Ps 119:66, 71, 75, 91, 125, 130
• Lk 10:17-24

4 Saturday

Love God above all, so that warmed by his embrace you may be aflame with divine love.
—St. Bruno

5 SUNDAY
Twenty-seventh Sunday in Ordinary Time
• Is 5:1-7 • Ps 80:9, 12-16, 19-20 • Phil 4:6-9 • Mt 21:33-43

6 MONDAY
Saint Bruno; Blessed Marie-Rose Durocher
• Gal 1:6-12 • Ps 111:1b-2, 7-10 • Lk 10:25-37

OCTOBER

Through the rosary the faithful receive abundant grace, as though from the very hands of the mother of the Redeemer.
—Pope John Paul II

Our Lady of the Rosary
• Gal 1:13-24 • Ps 139:1b-3, 13-15 • Lk 10:38-42

7 Tuesday

• Gal 2:1-2, 7-14 • Ps 117:1b-2 • Lk 11:1-4

8 Wednesday

Eternal God, I offer you all my thoughts, words and actions of this day . . . for love of you, for your glory, to fulfill your divine will.

—St. John Leonardi

9 Thursday

Saint Denis and Companions; Saint John Leonardi

- Gal 3:1-5 • (Ps) Lk 1:69-75 • Lk 11:5-13

10 Friday

- Gal 3:7-14 • Ps 111:1b-6 • Lk 11:15-26

OCTOBER

> *[Jesus said:] "Blessed rather are those who hear the word of God and keep it."*
> —Luke 11:28

• Gal 3:22-29 • Ps 105:2-7 • Lk 11:27-28

11 Saturday

Twenty-eighth Sunday in Ordinary Time
• Is 25:6-10a • Ps 23:1-6 • Phil 4:12-14, 19-20 • Mt 22:1-14

12 Sunday

To pray well we need not speak much.
—St. John Vianney

13
Monday
- Gal 4:22-27, 31–5:1 • Ps 113:1b-7 • Lk 11:29-32

14
Tuesday
Pope Saint Callistus I
- Gal 5:1-6 • Ps 119:41, 43-45, 47-48 • Lk 11:37-41

October

You pay God a compliment by asking great things of him.
—St. Teresa of Jesus

Saint Teresa of Jesus
- Gal 5:18-25 • Ps 1:1-4, 6 • Lk 11:42-46

15 Wednesday

Saint Hedwig; Saint Margaret Mary Alacoque
- Eph 1:1-10 • Ps 98:1-6 • Lk 11:47-54

16 Thursday

*A Christian is not his own master,
since all his time belongs to God.*
—St. Ignatius of Antioch

17 Friday
Saint Ignatius of Antioch
- Eph 1:11-14 • Ps 33:1-2, 4-5, 12-13 • Lk 12:1-7

18 Saturday
Saint Luke, Evangelist
- 2 Tm 4:10-17b • Ps 145:10-13, 17-18 • Lk 10:1-9

October

*The cross is the way to paradise,
but only when it is borne willingly.*
—St. Paul of the Cross

Twenty-ninth Sunday in Ordinary Time
• Is 45:1, 4-6 • Ps 96:1, 3-5, 7-10 • 1 Thes 1:1-5b • Mt 22:15-21

19 Sunday

Saint Paul of the Cross
• Eph 2:1-10 • Ps 100:1b-5 • Lk 12:13-21

20 Monday

> *Behold, God is my salvation; I will trust,*
> *and will not be afraid.*
> —Isaiah 12:2

21 **Tuesday** • Eph 2:12-22 • Ps 85:9-14 • Lk 12:35-38

22 **Wednesday** • Eph 3:2-12 • (Ps) Is 12:2-6 • Lk 12:39-48

OCTOBER

> *My God, give me a zeal that is discreet and prudent, so that I may do everything strongly yet sweetly, gently yet thoroughly.*
> —St. Anthony Mary Claret

Saint John of Capistrano
- Eph 3:14-21 • Ps 33:1-2, 4-5, 11-12, 18-19 • Lk 12:49-53

23 Thursday

Saint Anthony Mary Claret
- Eph 4:1-6 • Ps 24:1-6 • Lk 12:54-59

24 Friday

God gave himself fully for us;
how can we not dedicate ourselves fully to God?
—St. Raphael Kalinowski

25 Saturday
- Eph 4:7-16 • Ps 122:1-5 • Lk 13:1-9

26 Sunday
Thirtieth Sunday in Ordinary Time
- Ex 22:20-26 • Ps 18:2-4, 47, 51 • 1 Thes 1:5c-10 • Mt 22:34-40

OCTOBER

*Let us ask the holy apostles Simon and Jude to help us know
and love the Master more each day,
and to follow him as the center of our lives.*
—Francis Fernandez

• Eph 4:32–5:8 • Ps 1:1-4, 6 • Lk 13:10-17

27 Monday

Saint Simon and Saint Jude, Apostles
• Eph 2:19-22 • Ps 19:2-5 • Lk 6:12-16

28 Tuesday

> *Put on the whole armor of God, that you may be able to stand against the wiles of the devil.*
> —Ephesians 6:11

29 WEDNESDAY • Eph 6:1-9 • Ps 145:10-14 • Lk 13:22-30

30 THURSDAY • Eph 6:10-20 • Ps 144:1b-2, 9-10 • Lk 13:31-35

OCTOBER

> *Great peace is with the humble man, but in the heart of a proud man is always envy and anger.*
> —Thomas à Kempis

- Phil 1:1-11 • Ps 111:1-6 • Lk 14:1-6

31 Friday

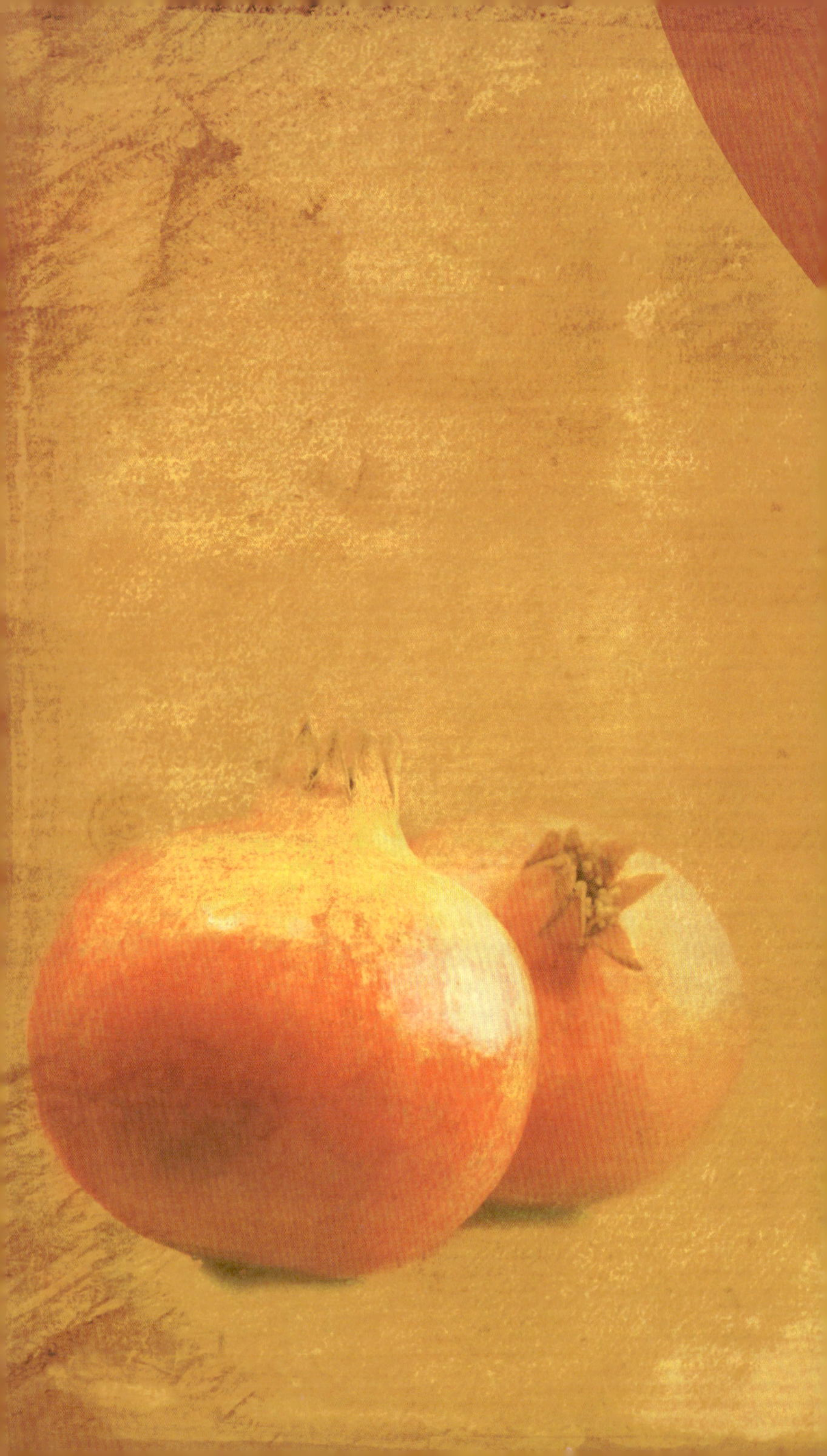

November

Christ made love the stairway that would enable all Christians to climb to heaven. Hold fast to it, therefore, in all sincerity, give one another practical proof of it, and by your progress, make your ascent together.

—St. Fulgentius of Ruspe

Make up your mind to become a saint.
—St. Mary Mazzarello

1 Saturday
All Saints
Not a Holy Day of Obligation
• Rv 7:2-4, 9-14 • Ps 24:1b-6 • 1 Jn 3:1-3 • Mt 5:1-12a

2 Sunday
The Commemoration of All the Faithful Departed (All Souls)
• Wis 3:1-9 • Ps 23:1-6 • Rom 5:5-11 or 6:3-9 • Jn 6:37-40

Be sure you first preach by the way you live.
—St. Charles Borromeo

Saint Martin de Porres
- Phil 2:1-4 • Ps 131:1-3 • Lk 14:12-14

3 Monday

Saint Charles Borromeo
- Phil 2:5-11 • Ps 22:26b-32 • Lk 14:15-24

4 Tuesday

NOVEMBER

Wait for the Lord; be strong, and let your heart take courage; wait for the LORD!

—Psalm 27:14

5 Wednesday

- Phil 2:12-18 • Ps 27:1, 4, 13-14 • Lk 14:25-33

6 Thursday

- Phil 3:3-8a • Ps 105:2-7 • Lk 15:1-10

I can do all things in him who strengthens me.
—PHILIPPIANS 4:13

• Phil 3:17–4:1 • Ps 122:1-5 • Lk 16:1-8

7 FRIDAY

• Phil 4:10-19 • Ps 112:1b-2, 5-6, 8-9 • Lk 16:9-15

8 SATURDAY

NOVEMBER

No one should be ashamed of the cross of Christ, through which the world has been redeemed.
—St. Leo the Great

9 Sunday
The Dedication of the Lateran Basilica in Rome
- Ez 47:1-2, 8-9, 12 • Ps 46:2-3, 5-6, 8-9
- 1 Cor 3:9c-11, 16-17 • Jn 2:13-22

10 Monday
Pope Saint Leo the Great
- Ti 1:1-9 • Ps 24:1b-6 • Lk 17:1-6

God would not urge us to ask, unless he were willing to give.
—St. Augustine

11 Tuesday
• Ti 2:1-8, 11-14 • Ps 37:3-4, 18, 23, 27, 29 • Lk 17:7-10

12 Wednesday
Saint Josaphat
• Ti 3:1-7 • Ps 23:1b-6 • Lk 17:11-19

November

Ingratitude dries up the fountain of divine graces. Give your tribute of gratitude often to the most loving Jesus.
—St. Frances Xavier Cabrini

13 Thursday
Saint Frances Xavier Cabrini
• Phlm 7-20 • Ps 146:7-10 • Lk 17:20-25

14 Friday
• 2 Jn 4-9 • Ps 119:1-2, 10-11, 17-18 • Lk 17:26-37

The greater and more persistent your confidence in God, the more abundantly you will receive all that you ask.

—St. Albert the Great

Saint Albert the Great
- 3 Jn 5-8 • Ps 112:1-6 • Lk 18:1-8

15
Saturday

Thirty-third Sunday in Ordinary Time
- Prv 31:10-13, 19-20, 30-31 • Ps 128:1-5
- 1 Thes 5:1-6 • Mt 25:14-30

16
Sunday

November

God does not require great achievements, but a heart that holds back nothing for self.
—St. Rose Philippine Duchesne

17 Monday
Saint Elizabeth of Hungary
• Rv 1:1-4; 2:1-5 • Ps 1:1-4, 6 • Lk 18:35-43

18 Tuesday
The Dedication of the Basilicas of Saint Peter and Saint Paul in Rome;
Saint Rose Philippine Duchesne
• Rv 3:1-6, 14-22 • Ps 15:2-5
• Lk 19:1-10 or Acts 28:11-16, 30-31 • Mt 14:22-33

Holy, holy, holy, is the Lord God Almighty, who was and is and is to come!

—Revelation 4:8

- Rv 4:1-11 • Ps 150:1b-6 • Lk 19:11-28

19
WEDNESDAY

- Rv 5:1-10 • Ps 149:1b-6a, 9b • Lk 19:41-44

20
THURSDAY

NOVEMBER

Ask Mary to lead you to Jesus and you will know what it is to live by his side.
—Cardinal Francis Xavier Nguyen Van Thuan

21 Friday
The Presentation of the Blessed Virgin Mary
- Rv 10:8-11 • Ps 119:14, 24, 72, 103, 111, 131 • Lk 19:45-48

22 Saturday
Saint Cecilia
- Rv 11:4-12 • Ps 144:1-2, 9-10 • Lk 20:27-40

> *God never abandons his people; indeed, he invites them to conversion so that his kingdom may become a reality.*
> —Pope Benedict XVI

Our Lord Jesus Christ the King
- Ez 34:11-12, 15-17 • Ps 23:1-3, 5-6 • 1 Cor 15:20-26, 28
- Mt 25:31-46

23 Sunday

Saint Andrew Dung-Lac and Companions
- Rv 14:1-3, 4b-5 • Ps 24:1b-6 • Lk 21:1-4

24 Monday

NOVEMBER

Lord, do your will and not mine.
—St. Alphonsus Rodriguez

25 TUESDAY
Saint Catherine of Alexandria
- Rv 14:14-19 • Ps 96:10-13 • Lk 21:5-11

26 WEDNESDAY
- Rv 15:1-4 • Ps 98:1-3b, 7-9 • Lk 21:12-19

In all created things discern the providence and wisdom of God, and in all things give him thanks.
—St. Teresa of Jesus

Thanksgiving Day
- Rv 18:1-2, 21-23; 19:1-3, 9a • Ps 100:1b-5 • Lk 21:20-28

27 Thursday

- Rv 20:1-4, 11–21:2 • Ps 84:3-6a, 8a • Lk 21:29-33

28 Friday

NOVEMBER

As the season for commemorating [Christ's] birth approaches, something stirs in us, something deep and profound, as if we are expecting a great miracle.

—Catherine Doherty

29 Saturday
- Rv 22:1-7 • Ps 95:1-7b • Lk 21:34-36

30 Sunday
First Sunday of Advent
- Is 63:16b-17, 19b; 64:2-7 • Ps 80:2-3, 15-16, 18-19
- 1 Cor 1:3-9 • Mk 13:33-37

Never pass a day without thanking Jesus Christ for all he has done for you during your life.
—St. John Vianney

NOVEMBER

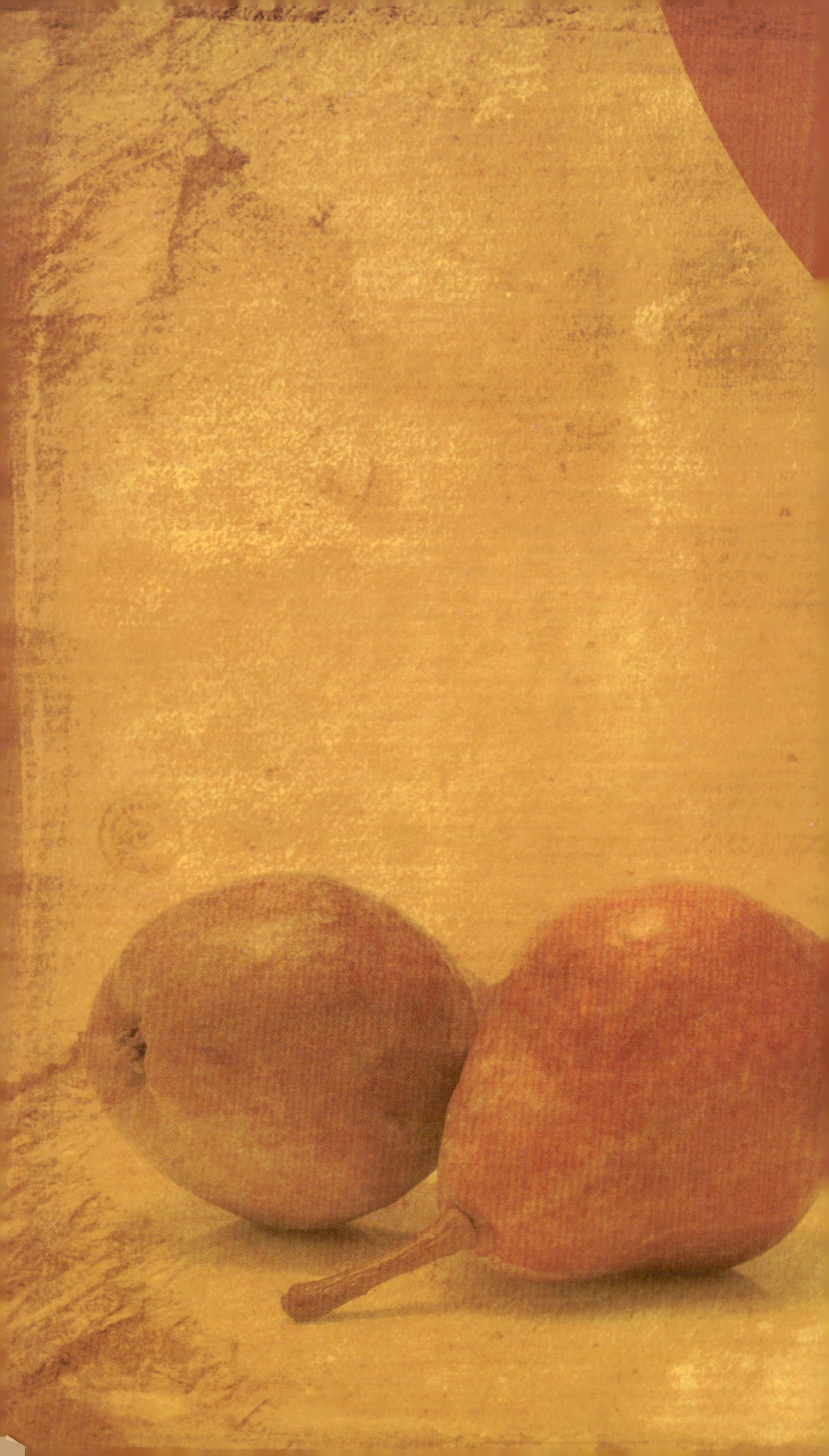

December

Put on then, as God's chosen ones, holy and beloved, compassion, kindness, lowliness, meekness, and patience, forbearing one another and, if one has a complaint against another, forgiving each other; as the Lord has forgiven you, so you also must forgive. And above all these put on love, which binds everything together in perfect harmony. And let the peace of Christ rule in your hearts.

—Colossians 3:12-15

The spirit of Advent largely consists in living close to our Lady during the time she is carrying Jesus in her womb.
—Francis Fernandez

1 Monday
- Is 2:1-5 • Ps 122:1-9 • Mt 8:5-11

2 Tuesday
- Is 11:1-10 • Ps 72:1-2, 7-8, 12-13, 17 • Lk 10:21-24

December

I earnestly pray you not to forget your own progress in virtue; for you are well aware that that one who does not make progress in virtue, goes backwards.
—St. Francis Xavier

Saint Francis Xavier
- Is 25:6-10a • Ps 23:1-6 • Mt 15:29-37

3 Wednesday

Saint John of Damascus
- Is 26:1-6 • Ps 118:1, 8-9, 19-21, 25-27a • Mt 7:21, 24-27

4 Thursday

Lord, do not let my heart lean either to the right or to the left, but let your good Spirit guide me along the straight path.
—St. John of Damascus

5 Friday
• Is 29:17-24 • Ps 27:1, 4, 13-14 • Mt 9:27-31

6 Saturday
Saint Nicholas
• Is 30:19-21, 23-26 • Ps 147:1-6 • Mt 9:35–10:1, 5a, 6-8

December

> *It is fitting that the Virgin should be resplendent with a purity such that none could be conceived more perfect except only God's.*
> —St. Anselm

Second Sunday of Advent
• Is 40:1-5, 9-11 • Ps 85:9-14 • 2 Pt 3:8-14 • Mk 1:1-8

7 Sunday

The Immaculate Conception of the Blessed Virgin Mary
Holy Day of Obligation
• Gn 3:9-15, 20 • Ps 98:1-4 • Eph 1:3-6, 11-12 • Lk 1:26-38

8 Monday

I am a compassionate mother to you and to all of my devoted children who will call upon me with confidence.
—Our Lady to St. Juan Diego

9 TUESDAY
Saint Juan Diego
• Is 40:1-11 • Ps 96:1-3, 10-13 • Mt 18:12-14

10 WEDNESDAY
• Is 40:25-31 • Ps 103:1-4, 8, 10 • Mt 11:28-30

DECEMBER

Hail, O Virgin of Guadalupe, Empress of America! Keep forever under your powerful patronage the purity and integrity of our holy faith on the entire American continent.
—Pope Pius XII

Pope Saint Damasus I
- Is 41:13-20 • Ps 145:1, 9-13b • Mt 11:11-15

11 Thursday

Our Lady of Guadalupe
- Zec 2:14-17 or Rv 11:19a; 12:1-6a, 10ab
- (Ps) Jdt 13:18b-19 • Lk 1:26-38 or 1:39-47

12 Friday

> *Every year Advent reminds us that grace—and that is God's will to save man—is more powerful than sin.*
> —Pope John Paul II

13 Saturday — Saint Lucy
- Sir 48:1-4, 9-11 • Ps 80:2-3b, 15-16, 18-19 • Mt 17:9-13

14 Sunday — Third Sunday of Advent
- Is 61:1-2a, 10-11 • (Ps) Lk 1:46-50, 53-54
- 1 Thes 5:16-24 • Jn 1:6-8, 19-28

December

> *From heaven he comes, the Lord and Ruler;*
> *in his hands are honor and royal authority.*
> —Advent Antiphon

• Nm 24:2-7, 15-17a • Ps 25:4-9 • Mt 21:23-27

15 Monday

• Zep 3:1-2, 9-13 • Ps 34:2-3, 6-7, 17-19, 23 • Mt 21:28-32

16 Tuesday

*Behold, a virgin shall conceive and bear a son,
and his name shall be called Emmanuel.*

—Matthew 1:23

17
WEDNESDAY

• Gn 49:2, 8-10 • Ps 72:1-4, 7-8, 17 • Mt 1:1-17

18
THURSDAY

• Jer 23:5-8 • Ps 72:1-2, 12-13, 18-19 • Mt 1:18-25

DECEMBER

> *[Mary said:] "Behold, I am the handmaid of the Lord; let it be to me according to your word."*
>
> —Luke 1:38

• Jgs 13:2-7, 24-25a • Ps 71:3-6b, 16-17 • Lk 1:5-25

19 Friday

• Is 7:10-14 • Ps 24:1-6 • Lk 1:26-38

20 Saturday

There is no other cause for the incarnation except this alone: he saw us bowed down to the ground, perishing, tyrannized by death, and he had mercy.
—St. John Chrysostom

21
Sunday

Fourth Sunday of Advent
- 2 Sm 7:1-5, 8b-12, 14a, 16 • Ps 89:2-5, 27, 29
- Rom 16:25-27 • Lk 1:26-38

22
Monday

- 1 Sm 1:24-28 • (Ps) 1 Sm 2:1, 4-8 • Lk 1:46-56

December

Fight all error, but do it with good humor, patience, kindness, and love. Harshness will damage your own soul and spoil the best cause.
—St. John of Kanty

Saint John of Kanty
- Mal 3:1-4, 23-24 • Ps 25:4-5b, 8-10, 14 • Lk 1:57-66

23 Tuesday

- Morning: 2 Sm 7:1-5, 8b-12, 14a, 16
- Ps 89:2-5, 27, 29 • Lk 1:67-79

24 Wednesday

Today Godhead pressed itself like a seal upon manhood, so that with the Godhead's stamp, manhood might be adorned.
—St. Ephrem

25 Thursday

The Nativity of the Lord (Christmas)
Holy Day of Obligation
- Is 52:7-10 • Ps 98:1-6 • Heb 1:1-6 • Jn 1:1-18

26 Friday

Saint Stephen, First Martyr
- Acts 6:8-10; 7:54-59 • Ps 31:3c-4, 6, 8ab, 16b-17 • Mt 10:17-22

DECEMBER

Parents by word and example are the first heralds of the faith with regard to their children.
—Vatican II, *Lumen gentium*

Saint John, Apostle and Evangelist
- 1 Jn 1:1-4 • Ps 97:1-2, 5-6, 11-12 • Jn 20:1a, 2-8

27 Saturday

The Holy Family of Jesus, Mary, and Joseph
- Sir 3:2-7, 12-14 or Gn 15:1-6; 21:1-3 • Ps 128:1-5
- Col 3:12-21 or Hb 11:8, 11-12, 17-19 • Lk 2:22-40

28 Sunday

> *For the name of Jesus and in defense of the church,*
> *I am willing to die.*
> —St. Thomas Becket

29 Monday
Saint Thomas Becket
- 1 Jn 2:3-11 • Ps 96:1-3, 5b-6 • Lk 2:22-35

30 Tuesday
- 1 Jn 2:12-17 • Ps 96:7-10 • Lk 2:36-40

December

> *New Year's Eve—this is the moment of beginning again, . . .*
> *the moment in which the old touches the new,*
> *in which we offer gratitude to God.*
> —Catherine Doherty

Pope Saint Sylvester I
• 1 Jn 2:18-21 • Ps 96:1-2, 11-13 • Jn 1:1-18

31 WEDNESDAY

Reserve Next Year's *Prayer Journal* Today!

The Word Among Us *2009 Prayer Journal*

Continue your journey of faith with next year's *Prayer Journal*. As always, you'll get inspirational quotes and a complete listing of the daily Mass readings, saints' feast days, and holy days of obligation. Give it as a gift and introduce a friend to the pleasures of journaling.

—Also Available—

Abide in My Word 2009—Mass Readings at Your Fingertips

Keep abreast with the daily Mass readings and make personal Scripture reading easier! *Abide in My Word* provides each day's Scripture readings in an easy-to-locate format. Each day is clearly listed so that it only takes a few minutes to draw near to the Lord through the Mass readings. Use it together with your *Prayer Journal*.

To order, use the card below or call **1-800-775-9673**

You'll find up-to-date product information on our Web site at www.wordamongus.org

Fill in the card below and mail in an envelope to:

The Word Among Us
9639 Doctor Perry Road, #126
Ijamsville, MD 21754

Order 2 or more copies and save 10%!

☐ **YES!** Send me _____ copies of the *2009 Prayer Journal*. JPRAY9
(1 @ $13.95; 2 or more @ $12.56 each plus s&h)

☐ **YES!** Send me _____ copies of *Abide in My Word 2009*. BABDE9
(1 *Abide in My Word* @ $16.50; 2 or more @ $14.85 each plus s&h)

☐ **YES!** Send me the *2009 Prayer Journal* **AND** 2009 *Abide in My Word* for only $27.60 plus s&h! 9SETA

Name _____
Address _____
City _____
State _____ Zip _____
Phone (_____) _____
E-mail (optional) _____

Send no money now. We will bill you.

SHIPPING & HANDLING (Add to total product order):				
If your subtotal is:	$0-15	$16-$35	$36-50	$51-75
Add shipping of:	$5	$7	$9	$11

CPPJ8Z